Illa. April 2007

SAMURAI

SELLING

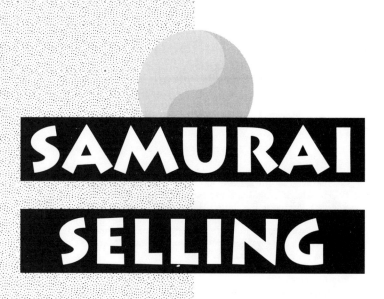

SAMURAI SELLING

THE ANCIENT ART OF SERVICE IN SALES

Chuck Laughlin
and Karen Sage
with
Marc Bockmon

St. Martin's Press
New York

Editor: George Witte
Design by Robin Hoffmann

Library of Congress Cataloging-in-Publication Data

Laughlin, Chuck.
    Samurai selling : the ancient art of modern service / Chuck
Laughlin, Karen Sage, Marc Bockmon.
        p.   cm.
    ISBN 0-312-11885-6
    1. Selling   2. Customer service.   I.   Sage, Karen.
II. Bockmon, Marc.   III.   Title.
HF5438.25.L38   1993
658.8´5--dc2   092–44201
                                                              CIP

First Paperback Edition: January 1995
10 9 8 7 6 5 4 3 2 1

This book is dedicated to our parents, Helen and John Laughlin, and Glen and Jettie Sage. We deeply love and appreciate your early guidance toward the values we live and express in this book.

To our children, Steve, Brad, Sandy, Kristin, and Charles. We love how you constantly teach us to keep "The Beginner's Mind."

To Garvin Lally. You will never be forgotten.

And finally, to all those sales people who possess the spirit of the Samurai. We recognize you for your intense sense of service to your prospects and your constant striving for excellence. This is the true path of the Sales Samurai.
—Chuck Laughlin and Karen Sage

To Marie, my samurai-spouse, who is not only "one who serves," but one who serves with joy.
—Mark Bockmon

CONTENTS

THIS IS NOT A BOOK ABOUT MARTIAL ARTS, but a book about <u>selling</u>. Through our work with dozens of major selling organizations and hundreds of professional salespeople, we are convinced that the modern salesperson can learn much from the ancient samurai about strategy, tactics, training, and mindset. *Samurai* means "one who serves," and we believe that service is the key to success in selling. In this book we'll give you hard and fast selling rules and illustrate the principles with stories drawn from the adventures of actual ancient samurai and modern samurai salesmen.

The authors are in favor of ending all vestiges of sexism in the workplace; we endorse equal opportunity, equal pay, and equal respect. However, as literary people, we find removing all gender from our language is not unlike making an apple box out of a desk—you can do it, but it isn't very efficient or effective, and it makes for extremely awkward reading. Therefore, we hope we will be forgiven for using *he* instead of the more cumbersome *he/she* or *she/he* if for no other reason than *he/she/she/he* when read aloud sounds more like laughter than communication. Also, when referring to our title character, we beg the reader's indulgence if we use *Samurai Sales<u>man</u>* instead of *Samurai Sales<u>person</u>,* as the former has a certain alliterative value that the latter lacks. Rest assured, however, that whenever we say "Samurai Salesman," we mean sales professionals of both sexes. After all, in ancient Japan, some of the most famous samurai were female!

We have quietly left behind the "me generation" with its selfish approach to living and have slowly begun to rediscover that serving others is, indeed, an essential part of a successful life. We seem to be returning to what earned us the freedom we enjoy today—to our tradition of finding meaning and adventure in serving others.

—Roberto Goizueta,
Chairman and CEO,
Coca-Cola Company

SAMURAI

SELLING

A TALE

OF TWO

SAMURAI

THIS IS A BOOK ABOUT *SELLING*, not a book about martial arts. More than that, it is a book about applying the secrets of the samurai to success in selling and in life. If your concept of samurai comes from watching comic John Belushi hack vegetables with a sword in the guise of "samurai chef" or from movie clips where a samurai walks about calmly severing limbs and heads, kindly erase those memories so that we may start afresh. *Samurai* is an old Japanese word meaning "one who serves," and therein lies the secret to your success as a *samurai salesman*—service. The samurai was not a maniac with a sword; he was a man with a mission that could be summed up by the question, "How can I best serve my client?"

Salespeople, like soldiers, react to an emergency or an unexpected event in one of two ways. If they've been highly trained, they react as they have been trained to react. If they have not been trained, they stumble around, ad-lib, and probably are destroyed by the other side. Knowing this, the samurai soldier trained himself so that his mind was as sharp as his sword, so he could survive in any situation. So must the samurai salesman.

The ancient samurai trained not merely for war but for a lifetime of service, not only to their client lords but to family, friends, and the community at large. This service brought them respect, honor, power, prestige, wealth, and happiness. It also made them indispensable to the one they served.

In this book we will examine the code of the samurai and see how it applies to selling situations. We will also share a few samurai stories to illustrate our points. Having been successful salespeople and sales executives, the authors realize that some of our readers will want to cut to the meat of the message. You'll miss a lot of the flavor, but we understand those who feel that way. Therefore, we have put our samurai analogies in gray boxes, so you can ignore them if you wish. It's your choice. Knowing the options and making the right choices are what being a samurai is all about. Let us begin by looking at two samurai—one in the seventeenth century and one in the twentieth.

A LESSON FROM THE SAMURAI

JAPAN, EARLY SEVENTEENTH CENTURY
Fifty samurai sat contentedly around the campfire, confident of the outcome of tomorrow's battle. From spies in the city, they had learned that their adver-

sary had been able to hire only one *ronin*, a freelance samurai, to meet their challenge. With the odds fifty-to-one in their favor, they knew tomorrow would not be a battle but an execution of the one man foolish enough to stand in their way. What they had not been told was that the samurai they would face was Musashi, the most famous and feared warrior in all of Japan.

Musashi stood in the shadows of the hill overlooking their camp. Their confidence was mirrored by their voices, by their laughter, by their songs—and by the fact that they hadn't even bothered to post sentries. Musashi knew the confidence they felt was false confidence, because it was not based on what they could do but upon what they thought their opponent would do. False confidence had cost many samurai their lives, many a warlord his kingdom. In spite of their numbers, Musashi also had confidence, but it was a true confidence based on his own abilities. It was a confidence born of years of learning his craft, studying his competition, learning to harness his thoughts and his actions so that he could react instinctively under pressure.

Musashi watched as his own servant entered the camp to tell the samurai that tomorrow they would face not an ordinary samurai but Musashi himself. A hush fell over the camp as they heard the words the servant spoke. Sentries began to move out into the darkness, and the others moved quietly to their tents to prepare for tomorrow's battle. The camp fires, now unattended, burned low, and a cloud moved in front of the face of the moon, plunging the valley into darkness.

Musashi turned and silently walked back into the woods. He could sleep soundly tonight, knowing that they would not. All night fear would gnaw at their courage, and they would awaken late, tired, and dispirited. Musashi smiled the smile of a master

samurai who is in control of the externals as well as
the internals. He knew that they would expect him at
midday by the tree near the rice paddy, where they
hoped to destroy him by sheer weight of numbers.
Musashi would meet them there—but not when they
expected him. Musashi never played the game exactly the way his opponents expected.

Musashi would need all his strength, skill, and
training tomorrow, but he was not worried. He had
learned long ago that when you had done all you
could do, it was best to put thoughts of failure out of
your mind and to concentrate on winning.

He was a master swordsman, "the way of the
sword." Musashi knew the way well, and he had
never lost a battle. Soon, other samurai began to
believe that he was invincible.

Tomorrow, however, he was not fighting a simple one-on-one duel but a battle. Two steel swords
hung at his waist. Like any master swordsman, he
was able to fight and defend from eight different
directions at once. More than that, he had practiced
each possible offensive and defensive move tens of
thousands of times and had the supreme confidence
of one who knows his craft better than his competitors. Under such circumstances he had written, "One
such man can beat ten." He had to beat fifty, but he
knew only three or at most four could face him at a
time. The way he looked at it, four-to-one odds gave
him a decided advantage!

In any battle the one with the best spirit and techniques has the edge. Musashi had developed a new
method of attack. He had taught himself to fight with
two long swords at once. He was so good at two-
handed swordplay that the right hand actually didn't
know what the left hand was doing. In effect, he was
as efficient as two master swordsmen. By his way of
reckoning, that reduced the odds to merely two-to-
one—hardly worth mentioning. So long as his

strength did not fail, he could beat innumerable opponents.

Fully as great as the other advantages Musashi had acquired over the years of his samurai service was his reputation. His adversaries knew him to be a man of great skill and high principle. The very mention of his name had brought fear into the camp, and he knew that by the time he attacked, fear would have reduced the competition by half and shaken the confidence of those who remained. He lay down to sleep, not at all worried about tomorrow.

AMERICA, LATE TWENTIETH CENTURY

Sheila Stephens entered the buyer's office and looked at the long line of salespeople waiting to get in. She did a quick count. Including herself, there were eleven competitors vying for *one contract,* and all presentations had to be made today. She walked confidently up to the receptionist and gave her name in a clear, steady voice. Out of the corner of her eye she noticed a couple of her competitors look up from their magazines. One nudged the other, who quickly put down his magazine and started rummaging in his briefcase for his presentation. Sheila smiled to herself. It was too late to practice and rehearse now; the curtain would be going up any minute.

Sheila took a seat in a corner by herself, where she could watch the others unobserved. Across the room from her was Charles Anderson, a salesman of the old school, a glad-hander with a repertoire of jokes. He was a "hip-shooter," one who never spent time on research and preparation for a sales call. Next to him was Frank

Elkins, a detail man, so enraptured with the technical whistles and bells of his equipment that he gave feature presentations, never stopping to realize that clients don't buy features, but *solutions*. Next down the line was Brenda Williams, who had beauty and poise but had never really learned her product line. She never deviated from her memorized presentation and her flip chart. To her left was Alex Wilson. Alex gave polished presentations, but since he never found out what specific problems his prospect wanted solved, he seldom hit the mark! Finally, there was Bubba Graham, an ex pro-football player whose name opened a lot of doors, but whose clumsy sales technique just as quickly closed them. A client had once confided to Sheila, "Bubba has more muscles in his *head* than most people have in their whole body!"

As Sheila thought about her competitors, her confidence soared. An ordinary salesperson who looked merely at externals would have said odds were ten-to-one against her. Sheila knew better. She could defeat four of her competitors in the first few seconds of her presentation. Another three would defeat themselves. That meant that only three were serious competitors. Three-to-one odds were well within the range of victory!

As a good samurai, Sheila not only knew her own company and products, she knew her competition. She had heard or read most of the sales presentations. She knew their equipment, their service records, their corporate and individual strengths and weaknesses. She had already done "mock battle" in her mind with each of them a hundred times. She had rehearsed and practiced so she could parry every thrust, respond to every challenge. She knew not only the features of her product but the benefits. More than that, she had taken the time to learn her prospect's wants and needs and had structured her presentation accordingly. Sheila had an unfaltering commitment to service for her clients, the true spirit of the samurai.

The receptionist called Sheila's name. She picked up her briefcase and walked confidently into the inner office, filled with the knowledge that she could defeat those who had made their presentations before her as well as make those who would come afterward pale by comparison. She was relaxed and at peace, yet poised and ready, the mark of a true samurai! Musashi would have been proud!

A LESSON FROM THE SAMURAI

JAPAN, EARLY SEVENTEENTH CENTURY

Miyamoto Musashi rose well before dawn and prepared himself for battle. Carefully he examined the edges of his swords. The sword of the samurai differed from the sword of the European swordsman. The European rapier was thin, designed to pierce rather than cut. The swordsman wielded it with delicacy and finesse. By contrast, the sword of the samurai was thick and sharp, composed of hammered steel folded so that it consisted of between thirty thousand and *one million layers*! The sword of the samurai was designed for slashing and cutting and was strong enough to cut through a pile of copper coins without nicking the blade or to lop the barrel off a modern machine gun! Thick leather armor could foil a European blade, but the samurai blade cut through armor and bone, severing limbs in a single stroke. A typical duel between European swordsmen took many minutes. A duel between samurai was measured in seconds, because the first mistake was the last.

Musashi drew his sword and looked at his reflection in the highly polished blade. He knew that his enemies considered him invincible, and their opinion was not without foundation. Once a master samurai had challenged Musashi to a duel, and on the way to the island where they were to meet, Musashi had carved a wooden sword from a paddle. When the boat had touched shore, Musashi had rushed toward his adversary with a fierce yell, wooden sword in hand. In a moment it was over, and the master with the sword of steel lay at the feet of Musashi and his sword of wood!

Musashi smiled at the remembrance. The rumor of invincibility was not true, of course, for even the greatest could be beaten by overconfidence or neglect of training. Yet he succeeded time after time by detecting weaknesses in his enemies while camouflaging his own. He often challenged his students with this question: "How do you keep from showing your weak point?" He answered himself by explaining, "By not babbling, loosely divulging information that can be used against you. You learn all about the opponent and *reveal only what is strongest about yourself.*"

He knew all about his opponents, but, just as importantly, he knew all about himself. He was ready. He walked to the woods near the plain where the battle would take place. Behind the plain was a rice paddy and beyond that more woods. He stood in the deep shadows and watched as the enemy, nervously waiting, took the field. He let them wait. Minutes passed as slowly as hours, and, finally, the hour appointed came and passed. One of the samurai on the field laughed and remarked to his friends that apparently the great Musashi had thought better of attacking fifty samurai and had crept away in the night. There was loud laughter, the kind that comes after danger has passed. While the laughter was still on their lips, Musashi drew both swords, gave a fierce yell and charged his adversaries! The nearest samurai grabbed his long sword and came out to meet him. Musashi watched his eyes, knowing the eyes are the windows of the spirit and the mind. Although the opposing samurai yelled menacingly and attacked with an air of fearlessness, Musashi could see the eyes showing fear. The eyes narrowed a bit before the man was ready to strike, and in that instant Musashi struck first. Having dispatched his opponent in less than two seconds, he engaged those on his right and left. He didn't bother with those behind, because Musashi was moving forward toward their leader, Yoshioka Hanshichiro. He knew that once he killed the shepherd, the sheep would scatter.

As he fought, each decision Musashi made was life or death, though he faced nothing today that he hadn't faced a thousand times in practice. Though a great number were arrayed against him, still only three, or at most four, could fight him at once. Each time he vanquished a foe, another took his place, but the replacement was a bit more frightened, a bit more apprehensive—and a bit less likely to prevail than his predecessor had been.

In less than two minutes Musashi and Hanshichiro stood face to face. Hanshichiro slashed with his sword. Musashi parried and lopped off his opponent's head, dispatching another enemy with the same stroke of the blade. Musashi dashed to the rice paddy, quickly dispatching three samurai who foolishly followed. He stood there a moment, but no one else came forward to face Musashi the Invincible. He laughed—and disappeared into the forest.

Musashi was pleased that he had served with honor. He had proven once again that one person who really knew the way of the samurai was of more value than a hundred who had merely studied the way. He had served well by always keeping the tools and techniques of his craft in good repair, by planning in advance, by analyzing the task at hand, by maintaining quiet confidence based on fact, by staying calm under pressure, and by performing at his peak.

He made a pot of tea, and as he sipped it, he contemplated the beauty of a bird as it flew among the trees, wondering if he should write a haiku poem about it. Once again Musashi had accomplished all that he had promised. No client can expect more than that.

AMERICA, LATE TWENTIETH CENTURY

Sheila Stephens made her presentation with the mindset of the samurai. She was calm, confident, and in control. She wasn't thinking about her next call or her last call, but about this call. She had trained herself to absorb the sounds, taste, and feel of the now. Living in the now wasn't a "sometimes thing" she did, but an "all times" thing she did. Wherever she was, whoever she was with, she gave her full, undivided attention.

As a samurai, she had forced herself to look at the fears she had created in her life: fear the prospect wouldn't see her, fear she wouldn't make quota. She had studied fear and found that it lived either in the past (what had happened) or in the future (what might happen)—and had no place in the here and now. Consequently, she had learned to banish fear, because fear diverts energy. Sheila knew fear stole the *now* moment by moment and took away mental clarity. In ancient Japan, lack of mental clarity meant certain death to a samurai. In modern America, lack of mental clarity meant certain death of a sale. In either case, fear exacted much too high a price to find a place in the mind of the samurai. It was easy to banish fear, because she wasn't focused on *her* problems or *her* needs but on *the prospect's* problems and needs.

Filled with confidence and a desire to serve, Sheila walked into the prospect's office with what Mark Twain called "the quiet confidence of a Christian with four aces." She knew both her prospect and herself and, therefore, had confidence that her product and service offered the solution the prospect needed. Because she knew how important finding the right solutions was to her prospect, she had a sense of urgency as she made her presentation. Once the prospect realized how her solutions fit his problems and saw that her desire to serve was genuine, he began to develop a sense of urgency about obtaining those solutions *now*!

Ten minutes later Sheila came out of the prospect's office. She smiled politely at her adversaries, who were still waiting to call on the prospect. It cost her nothing to be polite, because the battle was already over. As usual, the samurai had won.

Chapter 1: Self-Check Exercise
On Becoming a Samurai Salesman

1. In business battles, neither side takes prisoners. You either win—or lose—it all. Therefore, it is vitally important to your economic survival that you win as often as possible. In the twin scenarios we just gave, we looked at both an early-seventeenth-century and a late-twentieth-century samurai.

What common traits did you find?

Samurai Warrior	*Samurai Salesman*
_____	_____
_____	_____
_____	_____
_____	_____

2. The success of both the samurai warrior and the samurai salesman comes through service and problem solving. In the space below, write down your prospect's greatest problem, and detail how your product or service will solve it!

Prospect's problems:_____

_____

How this problem affects my prospect:___

_____

How my product or service will help solve the prospect's problem: _____

_____

_____

3. In the space below, write down the greatest advan-

tage your prospect will gain from doing business with you instead of a competitor. (Don't forget to include yourself as an advantage!)

_____

_____

4. How would you, as a samurai salesman, communicate that to your prospect?

_____

_____

5. What traits of the samurai are *easy* for you to use? Which ones are the most *difficult* for you?

_____

_____

To become a truly effective samurai salesman, it is not enough to think and feel like a samurai *some of the time*. You must think and feel like a samurai *all of the time*. How you do this is covered in the next chapter.

Memo from Musashi:
Make your combat stance your everyday stance and your everyday stance your combat stance!

2

THE

IMPORTANCE

OF KI

YOUR *KI* IS WHO YOU are on the inside.[1] It's who you are when no one else is around. It is you as you really are, without the camouflage, without the subterfuge, without the hype. It's the face you see in the mirror each day. In *The Wizard of Oz* the wizard presented himself as all-knowing, all-wise, and all-powerful. Yet when Toto pulled the curtain aside, Dorothy and her friends found

---

1. It is pronounced "key," and it is the key to your success in selling!

a frightened and confused little man who was insecure about his abilities. Deep inside, many of us sometimes feel like the wizard: a little bit insecure, a little bit confused, and a little bit incompetent. In a word, we have bad *ki*, a poor self-image. Unfortunately we can't help revealing it to others.

A LESSON FROM THE SAMURAI

The shogun invited master samurai Mitsuyoshi to give fencing lessons to his thirty-eight attendants. As the lesson proceeded, a messenger arrived from the Council of Elders. The shogun, thinking the messenger was one of his own retainers, ordered him to take a fencing lesson, too.

The messenger obediently picked up the wooden sword and took his place at the end of the line. Mitsuyoshi quickly defeated all of the attendants, looked at the messenger for a moment, and took his seat. He then asked the shogun, "I agreed to give lessons but not to have formal matches. Why did you hold back a man of such excellent ability as this last opponent? It does not become you." The shogun expressed surprise and apologized. How did Mitsuyoshi know that he faced another master? He sensed the ki of his opponent!

WHAT IS KI?

Ki is the blending of mind, heart, and spirit. Samurai believed there was a power that flowed through the universe and that they could tap into this power by being in harmony with it. They achieved this harmony by training their bodies and minds to focus only on what was truly important at that moment. They practiced until they could do this without conscious thought or mental strain. In fact, they felt that straining showed there was something lacking in their *ki*. When body, heart, and spirit were in harmony, others would sense this quiet confidence as a presence, as a power, and would retreat before it in awe.

As the great Musashi said, "You will be able to beat ten men with your *ki* alone! And once you have reached this point, will you not be invincible?"

Morihei Ueshiba, the founder of aikido, worked long and hard to perfect his *ki*. Once he accompanied a religious group to Mongolia, where they were ambushed by bandits with firearms. For a moment he expected to die against such odds, but then something strange happened. He relates, "When I concentrated my vision... I could see pebbles of white light flashing just before the bullets. I avoided them by twisting and turning my body, and they barely missed me. This happened repeatedly with barely time to breathe, but suddenly I had insight.... I saw clearly that the movements in martial arts come alive when the center of *ki* is concentrated in one's mind and body. The calmer I became, the clearer my mind became. I could intuitively see the thoughts, including the violent intentions, of the other."[2] How well he had mastered his father Morihei's lessons!

As Morihei grew older, his body inevitably weakened—but never his *ki*. In his late seventies he would often demonstrate against five or six adversaries at once. He invariably won these contests, explaining, "Regardless of how quickly an opponent attacks or how

2. Kisshomaru Ueshiba, The Spirit of Aikido (Tokyo and New York: Kodansha International, 1984), p. 38.

slowly I respond, I cannot be defeated. It is not that my techniques are faster...it has naught to do with speed. I am victorious right from the start. As soon as the thought of attack crosses my opponent's mind, he is already defeated regardless of how quickly he attacks."[3]

Morihei had learned, as we must, an ancient truth, that *ki*, the melding of mind, heart, and spirit, determines the outcome of a contest. In fact, if your *ki* is strong enough, others will sense it without your having to say a word, as Mitsuyoshi did that day in the hall of the shogun.

Recognizing the *ki* of another is not some strange psychic skill. We all have the ability to do it. The only difference between you and Mitsuyoshi or Ueshiba is that they practiced and polished their skills. Think back. Have you ever seen someone enter a room who could make their presence felt without saying a word? It was as if power radiated from them and touched you. That was their *ki*, their inner being, and it was affecting you! By the same token, we've seen people whose *ki* is so weak that when they enter a room it is as if someone had just left! Even animals can detect your *ki*. Dogs instinctively know if you like them or if you're afraid— and react accordingly!

A dramatic example of *ki* occurred during the freedom rally at Tienanmen Square in Beijing, China. When the government moved in tanks, many of the people scattered in terror. One nameless student, however, armed with no weapon except what looked like two shopping bags, blocked the lead tank. The tank swung left, and the student moved with it, extending the bags. The tank swung right, and the student stayed in front of the turret. The tank driver, armed with cannon and

3. John Stevens, *Abundant Peace* (Boston: Shambhala Publications, 1987), p. 112.

machine guns and the terrible weight of the tank, had his orders, and in the Chinese army to disobey was to die. The student was armed only with his *ki*. Can *ki* stop a competitor in his tracks? *Ki* can stop a tank!

Yes, we all know how the battle ended. Eventually the tanks attacked and ruthlessly murdered those who had rallied for freedom, but it is interesting to note that the attack came at night when soldiers could fire at faceless forms in the dark and not have to confront the awesome *ki* of the samurai student.

The secret to your success as a samurai salesman is to have the right ki.

What do you do if your *ki* doesn't radiate confidence, commitment, and caring? *Easy, you change your* ki. How do you do that? By thinking you are what you want to be. The author of Proverbs said, "As a man thinks in his heart, so is he." As Henry Van Dyke pointed out, the race doesn't necessarily go to the swift or the strong, but to the man who thinks he can! You change your *ki* by changing the way you think!

Because of the way they *think*, both the samurai warrior and the samurai salesman are able to stand against numerous adversaries who are equally or even better equipped. For the ancient samurai, *ki* became the inner power, the inner edge that they drew on not only in times of conflict, but moment by moment. Their *ki* showed in the face they presented to the world, because it was also apparent in the face they showed to themselves. It was who they really were, what they truly believed about themselves, and what they truly felt.

Many people spend a lot of time fashioning facades to impress others. Sometimes these facades include the pretense of caring, concern, service, knowledge, or power—but they are just that, pretenses, facades. A facade is as transparent as cellophane. Tesshu, one of the greatest samurai, developed the ability to read the *ki* of others so well that he frequently surprised his students by telling them what they were thinking. Tesshu was an expert at it, but most of us have the ability to look behind the words and see the inner person. This knowledge helps us know how to parry an attack or to anticipate an opportunity to serve.

A samurai never spends time building a facade to impress others but concentrates on building himself into what he wants to be. You can do this, too. Your *ki* is your value system, erected brick by brick. Those bricks are your education, your values, your ethics, your experiences, your religious beliefs, and your perception of who and what you want to be. Your *ki* is the foundation on which your integrity, sincerity, selling skills, and service rest.

In the final analysis most people see through facades, no matter how meticulously crafted, but your *ki*, who you really are, shines through. As Shakespeare wrote, "This above all: to thine own self be true, / And it must follow, as the night the day, / Thou canst not then be false to any man." If you're not right for you, you can't be right for your customers, either! When you're right for yourself, you're right with the world.

Recently, in one of our training sessions, a manager from the client company showed up and told the story of when he was an administrator of a hospital and Chuck Laughlin called on him. The administrator said, "After he left, I told my staff, 'You know, we're going to buy from him, but I don't know exactly why, because we really never got around to talking about the details of his system. There is something about his beliefs—something about who he is. Somehow I just knew that I'll be able to rely on him to provide a good solution and give good service.'" He was not responding to product features and benefits, but to Chuck's *ki*.

What is *ki*? When asked to describe the best salesperson who ever called on her, an executive summed it up this way, "I can't put my finger on just what it is about this person, but he has a *presence*."

One researcher interviewed a hundred salespeople who earned over $200,000 a year in commissions to see if he could discover what they had in common. He found that each believed his service was so important to the prospect that, if he lost the sale, the prospect lost, too! How would you react to a salesperson who wanted to serve you so badly that he felt he had rendered a disserve if he had failed to get the opportunity to serve you? Chances are, you'd buy from him, too!

Ki is **power**. In selling, your power is competence, your knowledge of the product, the market place, and, most particularly, knowledge of your prospects. You know what their problems are, what their goals are, and you have a willingness to work with them to find solutions.

Ki is **presence**. In selling, that presence is focused on your customer, allowing no distractions, no excursions, no hype. You are not worried about yesterday or concerned about tomorrow; you are in the here and now, listening, thinking, learning—helping them find ways you can serve them in the here and now.

Ki is **passion.** It is more than a message; it is a vision. If you are passionate about your cause and have a clear vision of where you and your prospect should be going, people will follow you. That's *ki.*

Think of someone you know who has strong power, presence, and passion. Study him.[4] Use him as a model. Look for clues to his *ki.* What do you see, hear, and feel that is extraordinary about him? Copy it!

Can't you feel the power of his *ki*? Surely you can—just as he can feel *yours.* Now, what can rob you of your *ki*? Obviously, since it is built on power, presence, and passion, lack of any of those essential elements robs you of your *ki.* When you let people begin to chip away at it,

4. We use "him" as a form of linguistic shorthand, realizing in half the cases the person you've chosen will be female.

it begins to disappear. Friends within the company can damage your *ki* with statements like "I used to think we had the best product, but now that our competitor has come out with their new one, I'm not so sure. We may be in real trouble."

When you start entertaining doubts, before you know it, you'll be using less powerful language to describe your company and products. Your tone of voice and body language will tell your prospect that you don't really believe all that you're saying. Left unchecked, this can turn a samurai salesman into an ordinary salesman just pitching a product.

Chuck and Karen recently interviewed six salespeople at a client's office with no knowledge of their annual sales. After the interview, the client said, "I'd like to see if you can rank these salespeople one through six, with one being the best performer!" With no consultation between them, both Chuck and Karen correctly ranked the salespeople. How? By sensing their *ki*!

How Customers See Through to Your Ki

Sales professionals spend a lot of time polishing their presentations, and that is time well spent. Yet one well-known study shows that only about 7 percent of our communication occurs through words. Thirty-eight percent of our communication is accomplished by the tonality of our voices, our inflections, and the subtle nuances in the way we speak. Fifty-five percent of our communication is nonverbal—our gestures, our facial expressions, and the way we sit or stand.

When we are face-to-face with a prospect, a tremendous amount of information about us, our products, and our services is being absorbed visually. If your *ki* is out of sync with your talk, it becomes obvious. When Chuck received a jury-duty summons, he was told, "Don't just listen to the words, but look very carefully at the people and how they're expressing themselves, because it is your duty to find the truth." The judge, in effect, was saying, "Listen to their words, but watch their *ki!*"

Why does your *ki* come through so clearly? Because communication is primarily under control of the subconscious mind. That's why it's true that as a man or woman thinks, so he or she is! Since this is true, there are only two ways to success. One way is to train yourself to become a pathological liar so your subconscious really doesn't know the difference between truth and fiction. That way, you won't be transmitting false signals. The other, better, simpler, more honorable way is to really believe in the truth of what you're saying.

If you believe in yourself and your product or service, your *ki* will be in sync with your words. When you talk about the service you will render, your gestures, your expressions, your tone of voice, and your entire being will echo, enhance, and magnify the message. Not only will the 7 percent of communication that takes place verbally be believable, but the 93 percent of communication that is nonverbal will be believable, too. The person to whom you are presenting will believe you at both a conscious and subconscious level because what you're saying and doing has a unified ring of truth.

The nonverbal power of *ki* is apparent even in the animal kingdom. When one dog approaches another for the first time, one immediately takes a subservient position, because the "boss dog" is obviously in charge—even if he is older, smaller, and weaker. In the same way, if your *ki* is right, there's a quiet confidence that's transmitted to everyone around you. You command respect, friendship, and trust. Your desire to serve will be obvious; your belief in yourself and the product or service you sell will come through. You don't have to believe your product is "the best." No product or service rates "best" on all scales. What you have to believe is that, by providing the service of a samurai, you can construct solutions for your prospects that will give them what they need. You must know that selecting your company will make the prospect's life better. You can be proud of something like that, and your prospect will sense your *ki* and buy.

But what if you don't believe that? Suppose you really think your product or service isn't any better than (or as good as) the competition's? Suppose you secretly don't want to serve at all. You just want to get the order, take the money and run. If those thoughts are in your *ki*, they will come out. Oh, any salesman can avoid *saying* those things, but if the thoughts are in your mind, they will be communicated anyway. If you honestly feel your product and services aren't right for the prospect, you should state that and get out! Don't waste your time or the prospect's if you can't be of genuine service. Only work with those for whom you can offer true service as a counselor, advisor, and friend—which is the way it should be anyway. Saying, "I'm sorry, but my product or service isn't right for you!" is a way of providing superior service. And providing superior service is at the heart of the true samurai.

A LESSON FROM THE SAMURAI

Makoto Sugawara, in *Lives of Master Swordsmen*,[5] tells of the time Musashi entered the service of the Lord Tadatoshi. The day he arrived at the palace, Musashi walked through the anteroom where his lord's samurai were awaiting orders and entered the audience chamber. Tadatoshi asked, "What do you think of my samurai?"

5. Makoto Sugawara, *Lives of Master Swordsmen* (Tokyo: Far East Publications, 1988), p. 72.

Musashi said, "There are many excellent samurai among your retainers, but one has attracted my attention far more than any other."

Tadatoshi was amazed that Musashi had selected one of the lower-ranking retainers but sent for him anyway. When the lower-ranking samurai arrived, Musashi said to him, "Your lord has ordered you to commit *seppuku* (suicide). Go to another room and prepare yourself."

The young samurai didn't flinch or hesitate, but bowed before his lord, rose, and retired to make preparations. Musashi then turned to Tadatoshi and said, "As you see, he is an admirable samurai, ready to accept death at any moment." Tadatoshi then recalled the young samurai and elevated him in position.

"What attracted you to him? And how so quickly?" Tadatoshi asked.

Musashi replied, "This one surpasses all others in alertness and sharpness of mind and body. Such thorough attentiveness can be possessed only by those who have totally internalized the spirit of the samurai and are ready to serve unflinchingly, whatever it costs!"

If your *ki* is right and you genuinely want to serve at all costs, you can defeat competitors who have better brand names, bigger resources, and better prices. If you, as a salesperson, can develop this *ki* to the point where you truly believe that your products and services are not only a solution but the best solution to your prospect's problems, then you will feel that you have failed your prospect if you don't persuade her to buy! At that point, you have become almost invincible!

During the attempted coup in the Soviet Union,

tanks were called in to surround the government building in which Boris Yeltsin and others in the pro-democracy movement were officed. Their orders were to open fire and, particularly, to kill Yeltsin. Yeltsin came out, climbed up on a tank, and thanked the tank commander for coming over to his side. A news report later quoted the tank commander as saying, "We *hadn't* decided to come over to his side, but he was so confident and so commanding that when he left, we talked it over and decided to join him!" What stopped the tanks? What brought democracy to the Soviet Union? A samurai named Yeltsin—with no weapon but his *ki*!

A LESSON FROM THE SAMURAI

The week before the great samurai Tesshu died of stomach cancer, he called all his trainees to his *dojo* (training facility) and told them to attack him with full force. They were all samurai, studying under the master samurai, and since that was the service he required, the seven or eight pupils attacked him with all the skill they possessed. At the end of the battle, only Tesshu was standing. Dying, his physical strength gone, he proved that his swordsmanship was a thing of the spirit.[6]

People are naturally attracted to a person with a wholesome, positive *ki*. Once you develop it, they will willingly trust themselves in your hands, knowing you'll hold

6. Adapted from John Stevens, *The Sword of No Sword* (Boston: Shambhala Publications), p.40.

and not hurt, support and not squeeze. Can you imagine the power you have when you have that kind of *ki* working for you? One salesman we know had the president of the prospect firm come over and hug him after an initial meeting, saying, "I want to tell you the difference between you and the other vendors. With them, I feel like I'm one of their prospects. With you, I feel like we're on the same team, just sitting down and working together to solve my problems." Can you imagine how much power you have with that prospect? Can you envision how difficult it is for an *ordinary salesman* to compete against a *samurai salesman* like you?

If you closed the book now and did nothing more than work on your *ki*, you would have gotten your money's worth. *Ki* makes the difference between good salespeople and great salespeople!

BUILDING A BETTER KI

How do you build a better *ki?* The first step involves your products and services. Do you *really* believe that your products are as good or better than anything the competition has to offer? Do you really believe your service is as good or better than theirs?

Often salespeople have a mistaken idea about the strength and ability of their competition. You see, you know your own operation inside out—so you know all the blemishes. On the other hand, all you know about your competition is what they want you to know. If you focus on the flaws in what you're selling, it's easy to fall victim to competitive propaganda and believe that what they sell is flawless.

Remember, Musashi often counseled his students to learn all they could about an opponent and to *reveal only what is strongest about themselves*. As you learn about your competitors, don't be fooled by appearances. Learn what they're really like.

Are you eating competitive propaganda like it was breakfast cereal? Do you find yourself looking for areas where your product is weak? Do you convince yourself that your price is too high, your service poor? If you begin to dwell on negative thoughts, then you contaminate your *ki* and lessen your chance of success.

How do you overcome this? List the strengths of your product or service and concentrate on those. Then list where your opponents are weak and vulnerable and think on those. You won't use their weaknesses for negative selling, but the quiet knowledge that the competition isn't all they're cracked up to be will give you confidence in your ability to defeat them.

Imagine, if you will, that you are standing with Musashi just before he goes into battle. He draws his sword and looks thoughtfully at the blade. "There are a lot of nicks in there," he mumbles. "I've heard that the competition uses better steel than we do. I also understand that their sword-sharpening service is better. I sure hope I don't have to use this thing, because I'm not certain if...." Get the drift? Musashi never did that, of course, because he was a samurai. He didn't even need a supersharp, steel-bladed sword. Wood would do well, because he had a supersharp *ki*!

Have you ever gone into a presentation focusing on the nicks? If you go into battle looking at the nicks in your own sword, you may not even notice when the competition hacks you to pieces with his sword (which is full of nicks)!

BUT WHAT IF THE NICKS
IN YOUR SWORD ARE SERIOUS?

No one is suggesting that you should try to convince yourself that placebos will cure cancer or that faulty products are the perfect solution for your client's real-world problems. If there are serious nicks in the product or service you offer, you need to get them fixed. (If you can't get them fixed, then consider switching to a company you can represent with pride.) Let us share how one major client solved the problem of nicks in the swords of their samurai salesmen!

This particular company had built a reputation on the basis of service, but lately service had been slipping, and, of course, sales were decreasing, too. In a sales meeting, one of the salespeople raised her hand and asked, "How can I sell in good conscience when I know that once I close the deal, the client won't be properly serviced?"

The sales staff agreed with her and decided that they could either accept deteriorating service as a fact of life or do something about it. Since these were samurai salesmen, their choice was clear. The question was, *what* could they do? After much discussion, they decided they would become the client's advocate. In other words, each salesperson could go to a prospective client and say, "When you buy our product, you not only get the solutions you need, but you get me to fight for you and to make certain this will work for you and that you will be properly serviced!" They drew up a mission statement right then that expressed determination to "achieve market dominance through *legendary service*." They were giving *lousy* service, but their goal wasn't good service or better service or even great service, but *legendary service*—a quantum leap over the competition. They drafted the mission statement, making forty-five copies, and they each signed all the copies.

Results came immediately. First, sales performance improved. A fundamental change in their *ki* made them mighty instead of meek, fearless instead of fearful, *one who serves* instead of *one who sells*. They knew going in that they would sell that prospect because they had the solutions and the services the client needed. The second thing that happened was that service began to improve. And why not? What service manager can withstand forty-five samurai salespeople who have just signed an oath in blood that they will fight to see that their clients get *legendary service*? Would Bambi challenge Godzilla to a duel? Just as Babe Ruth pointed to where the ball would go and put a home run in that exact spot, these salespeople pointed toward legendary service and drove straight toward the goal.

These salespeople had the soul of the samurai. They knew there are always nicks in the sword, and they were prepared to overlook minor ones. Yet, when the nicks got so bad that the success of their mission was in jeopardy, they repaired them. Good as new? No, better than new!

By the way, we don't like sales stories that don't have happy endings. The company with the forty-five samurai who made a commitment to legendary service turned a rapidly deteriorating sales effort around. They've enjoyed a 40-percent increase in sales in the twelve months since the meeting took place!

DON'T LET ANYONE
STEAL YOUR KI

You have worked hard to build your *ki*. Don't let any-one steal it! Bear in mind that the mind of the samurai is as sharp and hard as the blade of his sword. No one can take your *ki* by force, but they can take it by stealth. How? By eroding your confidence in your product, your service, and your self.

Co-workers can steal your *ki* by complaining about the company or by complaining about the problems without being willing to become part of the solutions. Either convert them or ignore them.

Competitors can steal your *ki* by undermining your confidence, telling you what's wrong with your product while concealing problems with theirs. Let them talk.

Learn all you can about their products, problems, and prospects while sharing nothing about yours.

You can steal your own *ki* by not qualifying prospects before you begin the selling process. You steal it by doubting yourself, by worrying about your product and the competition instead of worrying about how to solve the prospect's problems.

When you answer an objection with a strong, confident *ki,* the answer is accepted. If your *ki* is weak, no matter what your words, your answer is suspect. Anytime you make a key point, or answer a question, if you want it to be heard and believed, do it with a strong *ki. Step into your answer with ki!* When we give workshops on how to give powerful product demonstrations or sales closes, *ki* is often the only difference between a weak and ineffective presentation and a strong, powerful, sales-enhancing one!

Kisshomaru Ueshiba's maxim to live by was, "When *ki* takes leave, death ensues." In selling, we aren't talking about the death of a salesman (to borrow from Arthur Miller), but the death of a sale! To lose your *ki* is to die. A salesperson with a weak *ki* is a liability to the company. On the other hand, a salesperson with a strong *ki* is a fierce competitor and virtually unbeatable.

If you are sincere in your search for solutions, what does it matter if your solution has a few nicks in the blade? What does it matter if the competition has a shinier sword or a sword of finer steel? Musashi fought and won with a wooden sword against numerous master swordsmen armed with swords of steel! It is the *samurai* and not the *sword* that counts! Swords are merely tools. Battles are won with *ki!*

As the great samurai Tesshu wrote,

> *If your mind is not projected into your hands, even ten thousand techniques will be useless.*[7]

7. Stevens, *The Sword of No Sword,* p. 147.

When your thoughts, your *ki,* are right, clients and competitors will sense it, and doors and hearts will open to you, and competition will shy away from giving you battle. That's why *ki* is the secret of success for the samurai salesman.

Chapter 2: Self-Check Exercise On Developing Your *Ki*

1. What is your *ki* now? How would you describe your mental state when it comes to representing your products, your services, and yourself?

   My product *ki.*

   My service *ki.*

   My personal *ki.*

2. Now describe your *ki* as you'd like it to be:

   My product *ki.*

   My service *ki.*

   My personal *ki.*

3. What is the weakest link in my *ki?*

4. How can I strengthen my *ki* to make myself invincible?

5. Where is my competitor's *ki* the weakest?

6. In what ways will you have failed your prospect if you fail to persuade him to use your product or service?

7. *Ki* shows up as power, presence, and passion. What can you do to build your *ki and to make yourself a samurai salesman?*

3

THE

POWER

OF BALANCE

DURING THE LONG COLD WAR many speeches, papers, and books were written on the balance of power. Balance of power meant that opposing sides were so evenly matched that neither was tempted to launch an attack on the other. The Samurai understood the concept of balance of power, but he also understood a far greater concept—the power of balance.

The samurai knows that a successful sales career and a successful life can only come by balancing four virtues:

- Integrity
- Discipline
- Creativity
- Fearlessness

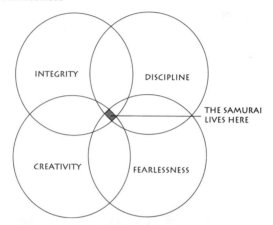

These virtues, driven deep in a bedrock of your *ki* or self-image, form four pillars of success. Let's look at each separately.

INTEGRITY

The first American dictionary, published in 1828, probably still provides the best definition for integrity: *"Integrity* comprehends the whole moral character, but has a special reference to uprightness in mutual dealings, transfers of property, and agencies for others." More modern sources give *honesty* for a synonym. At the bottom line, integrity means being true to your vision and purpose.

Integrity shows up in a lot of ways. Honesty is a given. Commitment is inherent. But genuine integrity shows itself in subtle ways, as well.

Not long ago, Black Mountain Spring Water Company made a decision to limit their geographical expansion because, even though they could deliver the product, they were growing so fast that they could not deliver the service they wanted. It was a tough decision, but management explained it this way, "To provide the kind of service we promised our customers, we had no other choice. A company of integrity can never promise more than it can produce."

This is an important lesson for a samurai. Keep your integrity by never promising a customer more than you can produce! Another way you can guarantee integrity in your relationships is to ask yourself, "What would I do if this person were a family member?" If you can't help a prospect, do both of you a favor and tell him. If you can, don't lie; don't even exaggerate. Live inside your integrity. It feels good, and it's a source of your *ki*. There is a line we like in an old Marlon Brando movie: "Every word I say is a promise." Now *that's* integrity.

A LESSON FROM THE SAMURAI

When Lord Asano presented a gift to his superior, Lord Kira, Kira thought that the size of his gift was too small and was insulted. Asano rose to challenge him, but Kira's troops subdued him, and he was ordered to commit *seppuku*. Having no other choice, Asano took his dirk and committed suicide. The forty-seven samurai who had served him sadly took him home to be buried—only to find that the estate had been confiscated by Kira.

The samurai sense of integrity did not permit this brutal murder to go unpunished. Yet Asano's samurai realized that Lord Kira had far too many samurai for them to best him in battle. Besides, Kira was expecting revenge and was waiting for them to strike.

Asano's samurai, therefore, hatched a plan to lull Kira into a false sense of security. Unemployed, they began to live like bums. To throw Kira off guard, Oishi, who had been Asano's chief retainer, began drinking and even divorced his wife of twenty years. After many days one of Kira's men found Oishi passed out in a gutter and stepped on his face and spit at him in contempt. Oishi merely grunted and rolled over, apparently unable to arise and take offense.

Kira relaxed his guard, feeling that those who might have taken up their client-lord's cause were no longer any threat. After all, over a year had passed, and Asano's men were no longer even fit to be called samurai. It was then that Oishi and his men struck. They stormed the palace, slew the guards, and found Lord Kira cowering in a closet. They commanded him to commit *seppuku*, and when Kira refused, they killed him with Asano's dirk.

Did they get away with it? Yes and no. They were sentenced to death, as they expected to be, but for the samurai, integrity of service meant more than life. They were buried with full honors beside their slain master.

As tough as the sales profession is, no one expects our sense of integrity to result in loss of life. However, the samurai code of taking care of one's client regardless of cost has applications even for our more civilized era.

A Modern Integrity Story

Craig Lacy, a friend who was once an independent insurance agent, prided himself as a person of integrity. Whenever he placed an insurance policy, he always tried to find the best value for his customer's premium dollar. He placed several policies with a third-party administrator who was backed by a highly respected insurance company. The insuring company discontinued their coverage, but the third-party administrator didn't notify the agents, choosing instead to continue to collect the premiums and pocket them. The third-party administrator then disappeared, taking the premiums with him, which sparked an FBI investigation.

By the time Craig discovered what had happened, two of his policyholders had outstanding claims, one a dentist with $1,500 worth of unpaid claims, and another a young couple who had a child by Cesarean section with an $8,000 bill. The attorney general of the state declared the offering fraudulent but held the insuring agents blameless. Craig had no obligation to offer anything but condolences. Instead, he paid the claims out of his own pocket!

Was Craig legally obligated to do anything? No. Was he morally obligated? Probably not, since he had acted in good faith. Yet, he did what he did because he is a person of integrity, and felt that the customers had bought Craig Lacy first and the policy second.

Incidentally, though Craig did what he did because he felt it was the right thing to do and for no other reason, the dentist became one of his biggest boosters. Craig later sold forty policies to other dentists who had been told by his first client, "Here's a guy who has integrity and will stand up for you, *regardless of cost!*"

John Frederick, chairman of Cameo Coutures, the largest direct-selling lingerie company in the world, shares the antithesis of Craig's story. John says, a former employer of his had made a commitment and wanted to wiggle out. "I'm not going to go through with this," the boss thundered, "and no one can give me any good reason why I should!" John told him, "I can give you a very good reason why you have to do it—*you gave your word!*" John adds, "He was quiet for a moment, then he said, 'Yeah, but I wouldn't have given my word if I'd known it would turn out like this!' I quit right after that, because I realized he was serious. His word meant nothing, and I knew a salesman with no integrity could never remain successful."

Integrity is one of the pillars of success. Yet, as important as integrity is, it cannot stand alone. It must be anchored to discipline.

DISCIPLINE

Every spectacular achievement is preceded by unspectacular preparation. No samurai can expect to achieve great things without preparation. When a quarterback scores a winning touchdown, when a salesperson makes a spectacular presentation, when samurai like Musashi defeat dozens of adversaries single-handedly, they are only doing publicly what they have prepared for privately.

You've heard the old adage, "Practice makes perfect." A good case in point is that rodeos grew out of a desire on the part of cowhands to show off the skills they had developed, practiced, and used every day out on the range. Their spectacular performances in the rodeo arena were made possible by unspectacular preparation day in and day out. The more you practice, the more you prepare, the better you'll be. If you want to be the best you can be, you must develop discipline.

Discipline, like integrity, is one of those words we all are "pretty sure" we can define. But can we? Want to take a turn at defining it? Go ahead, write your definition in the space below:

discipline: _____

_____

If you're like most of us, your definition had to do with *punishment* or *regimen*. It may surprise you to learn that the *first* definition of discipline is "teaching, learn-ing." The second definition is "instruction, a subject that is taught, a field of study." The third is "training that corrects, molds, or perfects the mental faculties or moral character." Discipline comes from the Latin word *disci-plina*, from which we also get the word *disciple*, meaning student or pupil.

Discipline, then, is learning and training, being a disciple of a person or a philosophy you wish to follow. If you served as a soldier in the armed forces, you were taught discipline in basic training. The best samurai sol-diers and salesmen are always those who impose *self-*discipline that is more stringent than any imposed by others.

The true samurai salesman is self-disciplining, be-cause he or she is so committed to serving company and customer that only the best is good enough. That means that a samurai practices his or her presentation every day—*whether anyone is watching or not*. It means he does it even if he's already an acknowledged master samurai like Musashi.

If you are prone to be a bit undisciplined, there is a cure for it: commitment. If you aren't committed to your goals, not only are you not a true samurai, you're just taking up space in your organization! How do you make commitment an integral part of your life?

A client company has a super-samurai who always triples the quota given him. We asked him how he does it, and he replied, "It's simple. On the day the quotas come out, I always publicly announce to management that I'm going to triple mine. Once I've made that com-mitment public, I have to do it, or I lose face!"

See how his *self-imposed* discipline worked for him? He would have considered himself a failure if he had come in at 50 percent over quota, even though other salesmen were satisfied to come in at 50 percent of quota.

When you make a public commitment, you're setting in motion powerful forces deep within your mind. If you follow that commitment with integrity and exhibit the discipline of a samurai, you'll find that your performance matches your practice, time after time.

Earlier, we talked about not letting anyone steal your *ki*. It's equally important that you not let anyone or anything erode your discipline. Discipline can be stolen by co-workers through envy ("You don't have to work that hard, Sheila. You're already top salesperson in the company!").

Any samurai can handle a threat from outside. The toughest threats are those from within. The biggest obstacle you'll have in building discipline is a tendency toward laziness. Even the sharpest mind or sword may grow dull with neglect, and the finest salesperson can begin to slip if he doesn't keep his skills sharp. Master violinist Isaac Stern puts it this way, "If I don't practice for a day, I notice it. If I don't practice for two days, the critics notice it. If I don't practice for three days—*everyone notices it!*"

When a samurai soldier, or a samurai salesman, begins to neglect the training and instruction that made him great, soon he will notice that his performance isn't quite so good as it had been, and eventually, everyone else will notice, as well. Remember: When unspectacular preparation ceases, eventually, spectacular results will cease, too!

A Modern Samurai Confesses Sloth

We've all known some undisciplined salespeople, folks who always seem to put more time into making excuses than they put into making sales. What we sometimes fail to realize is that even the best of us can slip into slothful habits. Chuck Laughlin recalls, "One place where I worked required all salespeople to turn in a loss report explaining why we didn't make the sale. It was designed as a learning tool so that we'd see what we had done wrong and learn to avoid the same mistakes in the future. Pretty soon, instead of a learning tool, that report became an excuse tool. I'd write down, 'I lost because the price was too high'; or 'I lost because our product was weak.' Suddenly I realized that the key words in each excuse were, 'I lost!' Why had I lost? I realized that *I lost because I was outsold!* Boy, that burned me up! How could I be outsold? I was the top salesperson in the company. I'd just gotten a bit lazy.

"I was in the process of writing the loss report when I realized that the only genuine excuse for my not getting the contract was that I was outsold. I didn't like to be outsold, so I went back to that client and asked him why I had lost. He told me that they liked my product but that they liked the competitor's price better than mine because his was turn-key. (*Turn-key* means a complete package with everything included.) I got my company to agree to let me present the prospect with two contracts. I told the prospect, 'You can sign the original contract that I designed for you or the turn-key one.' Then I explained why they didn't want the turn-key contract. *They signed the contract they had originally turned down!* I made the sale and made the client happy. And that was a lesson to me. From then on, I took full responsibility for my losses. When I did away with excuses for failure, I repeatedly came in at 300 percent of quota!"

A lazy salesperson accepts a loss gracefully, saying, "Oh, well, you can't win 'em all. Even Babe Ruth struck out 3,600 times!" A samurai salesman has a hard time rationalizing defeat because he hates to lose. After all, losing means that he didn't get a chance to serve, and the client didn't get what was best! Faced with these options, when the samurai appears to be losing, he redoubles his efforts and snatches victory from the jaws of defeat.

Sometimes it's even possible to win after you lose, as Chuck did when he realized that he had been outsold. Colonel Sanders did the same thing when he found himself sixty-five years old and the owner of a small café. One day he got his first Social Security check, and it made him angry. "It's as if the government were telling me, 'You're washed up; you're through; you've done all that you can do,'" he said. "And so I got to thinking about what I could do, and I decided that I could cook chicken better than anyone else, and I began franchising my recipe!"

So, you lost the deal. So, go back and ask why you lost. Go back and smile and politely ask what it will take to get the business. The key words are *Go back*! If you are a true samurai, wanting to serve, the client will be pulling for you and will be upset that you lost. We've seen that persistence can turn a loss into a win, and even if it doesn't, you'll learn something that will help you next time. Not even a samurai salesman closes 100 percent of the sales. But so long as each loss hurts—so long as each loss teaches you something—you're in no danger of becoming lazy. As Winston Churchill said, "Don't take no for an answer; never submit to failure." Samurai didn't have sayings like that. Laziness was not an option.

W. W. ("Foots") Clements, who sold his way from working on a Dr Pepper route truck to being president of the Dr Pepper Company, says, "Success is never final, and neither is failure unless you let it be."

Discipline Is a System

Discipline, whether it is a samurai practicing with a sword, an athlete working out with weights or a salesperson practicing a presentation, is a *system*. A system, in business parlance, is a variety of elements that work together to accomplish a goal. In a system, nothing is left to chance, but each element is designed to work with other elements to accomplish the objective. Examples are a telephone system, a software system, a plumbing system, a traffic control system, a computer system, etc. The implication of a system is that it is complete and that it continues to work. A system differs from a program in that a program (i.e., a space program, a TV program, an exercise program) has a definite start and a definite stop. A system goes on forever. (Wouldn't you hate to have a plumbing *program* or a telephone *program*? They would be no better than a discipline program!) Look for areas of your work and life where you lack discipline. Invariably, you'll find an inadequate system for creating the discipline and the success you need.

CREATIVITY

Discipline is about doing the basics until you have them down pat, like a musician practicing the scales. A lot can be accomplished by being methodical, but a lot more can be accomplished if we add creativity to the process.

A number of years ago, an ad man named Ben Duffy was president of BBD&O, one of the world's largest ad agencies. Ben heard through the advertising grapevine that Lucky Strike was looking for a new ad agency, so he called the president of American Tobacco and got an appointment. When Ben arrived, he said, "I got to thinking, if I were president of American Tobacco, what questions would *I* ask a new agency? So I made up a list of the ten most important ones that I thought you might like to have answered."

The president of American Tobacco said, "That's very interesting, Mr. Duffy, because right after your call, I did exactly the same thing. I made up my own list of ten questions. How would you like to trade lists?"

They did, and after a moment the president smiled and said, "As I see it, seven out of the ten questions on your list are also on mine."

Ben's creative approach and desire to serve got him the account. His creative edge? *Placing himself in the prospect's shoes!* As he began to think about what questions, concerns, worries, and hopes his prospect might have, he began to focus on just how he could answer those questions, ease those concerns, erase those worries, and fulfill those hopes.

People are always impressed with creativity. When we do something out of the ordinary, particularly if we are showing that we care, people notice. That creativity is part of our desire to serve. Learn to think "outside the box," that is, look at the big picture, not just the portion that concerns you. Solutions are often right in front of us if we'll only permit ourselves to look at problems from a different angle.

Lennox Industries, as part of their program to acquire new dealers, sends prospects a coffee mug and a pound of coffee with a note that they'd like to discuss options with them over a cup of coffee. National Gypsum company got started by enclosing a "Gold Bond" with each sheet of their gypsum wallboard, a tactic that not only increased sales but made "Gold Bond" wallboard a better-known name than the company that produced it! Dr Pepper got over a medicinal-sounding name by a creative campaign that capitalized on the uniqueness of the taste as well as the name—from "I'm a Pepper" to "Just what the doctor ordered!"

If you have the desire to serve, you will find creative ways to do it. When you think of solving a prospect's problems instead of selling your product, you have taken the first step in creativity. You'll find creative ways to say, "I care," "I'm capable," and "I'm concerned" to those you work with, work for, and love.

FEARLESSNESS

When a Medal of Honor winner was being praised for being fearless, he laughed and said, "I was always afraid. I simply learned that I could not let fear keep me from doing my job." All of us are fearful or, at least, apprehensive at times. Yet people do not buy from fearful representatives. (As a deodorant ad says, "Never let 'em see you sweat!") How do you eliminate fear? By eliminating ignorance! Fear, you see, is based on ignorance. We naturally tend to fear things in proportion to our ignorance of them.

To become fearless when facing competition or a client, you must know all that you can about your product, your competition, and your prospect. The more answers you know, the less you worry about the questions you'll be asked. With knowledge, "The only thing you have to fear is fear itself!"

You also banish fear by building up the other pillars of success: integrity, discipline, and creativity. The stronger your desire to serve (integrity), the harder you work to learn your product and your client's needs (discipline), the more thought you put into your presentation (creativity), the less afraid you will become.

A LESSON ON FEARLESSNESS FROM THE SAMURAI

In 1867 the great samurai Tesshu joined the personal guard of Shogun Tokugawa. A few months later, Tokugawa's palace was seized by Saigo, a commander for the emperor's troops. A brief civil war followed, but soon the imperial army overwhelmed Tokugawa's forces and advanced on Edo, prepared for one, last, bloody battle. Tokugawa's advisors favored waiting until the last minute before acting. Tesshu, on the other hand, felt that the time to negotiate was before the battle began and offered to go and negotiate with Saigo. In spite of warnings that it was too dangerous, he took the direct route right through Saigo's heavily armed sentries and reached Saigo's camp. "Continuing this war will destroy the country," Tesshu advised his adversary. "The emperor would not want our countrymen to be slaughtered."

Finally, Saigo agreed to end the fighting if Tokugawa would agree to four conditions:

1. Surrender of Edo Castle.
2. Evacuation of all troops from the castle compound.
3. Surrender of all weapons.
4. Tokugawa would be exiled to Bizen.

Tesshu said, "Please put yourself in my position. I have sworn allegiance and must do everything in my power to maintain my lord's honor. What would you do if you were in my position? I can't allow my lord to be exiled."

At last Saigo agreed and gave Tesshu a letter of safe conduct through his sentries, in spite of the fact that Tesshu had not needed one to reach him. As Tesshu turned to go, he saw some excellent horses. "Whose are those?" he asked. "The emperor gave them as a gift to the imperial forces," Saigo replied. "I am now one of those forces," Tesshu said, "for the war is ended!" He jumped on the finest of the horses and rode back to carry the good news to his master.[8]

We knew a sales manager who called his salespeople in and told them that they were going to lose a part of their territory if they didn't canvass it. One of the salespeople was livid. He was paid a $70,000 base, but he was terrified at the thought of picking up the phone and prospecting. He had gone through all the lazy exercises, trying to convince himself that this particular prospect

8. Adapted from Stevens, *The Sword of No Sword*, pp. 11–12.

didn't have the money, that one wasn't ready for the product, and that the other one had a special relationship with the competition. Finally, because he didn't want to lose part of his territory, he did the canvass, *and his sales shot up 50 percent!*

What are we afraid of? That someone will say no? (Or even, "Hell, no!"?) What's so terrifying about no? The worst that can happen is that you will find out they're not a prospect after all. That's great news! Now you can spend more time with real prospects. Can you imagine a samurai quaking before a possible no? Neither can we!

It took guts to be a warrior in the days of the samurai. They didn't fire missiles over the horizon at one another, or pick off an opponent from a quarter mile away with a sniper rifle. Samurai went out with swords and stood face to face with their opponents, and they *competed*. It took guts to be a samurai warrior, but the rewards were high.

The samurai salesman must have that same kind of tenacious courage, that same kind of fearlessness. The samurai is a bit ruthless when it comes to prepar-ing himself or herself for the contest. The samurai is also a bit ruthless when it comes to screening his prospect list.

The samurai believed in economy—economy of thought, economy of words, economy of effort. This showed up in their *haiga* painting and haiku poetry, art created with the minimum wasted motion. The samurai salesman must believe in economy, too.

For instance, a samurai salesman never invests his time in a prospect that is not worthy of his effort. If the client is not a valid prospect, if he doesn't have the imagination, the money, or the moxie, then find another prospect, no matter how much "fun" it is to call on that person, and no matter how much your boss wants the account. If he's not a valid prospect, pass on him and find one who is a valid prospect.

To catch fish, you must go where the fish *are*, not just to where it's pleasant to fish. The same is true with catching sales. Often, this means going into tough, difficult situations, which is why a spirit of laziness can never reside in the soul of a samurai.

THE POWER
OF BALANCE

The samurai succeeds because he balances his life on four sturdy pillars: integrity, discipline, creativity, and fearlessness. The samurai salesman lives in balance between these pillars, because that is the only way he or she can succeed. Salespeople who rely too heavily upon creativity may not discipline themselves and thus not get the results they desire. "I'll think of something," they'll assure themselves as they fall behind quota. They sell by the "seat of their pants." Salespeople who rely solely on discipline may strictly adhere to a prepared presentation and aren't able to react to creative openings when they appear. Salespeople who place too much stress on fearlessness and courage may neglect both discipline and creativity. And salespeople who rely only upon their integrity may neglect the other virtues and still lose the sale!

Success depends upon balance. A salesperson out of balance will always lose to one who is in balance. The samurai salesman in balance is a samurai who moves with power, because selling is a battle of the mind, not of products and pitches. In political circles, we hear about maintaining a "balance of power." Among samurai salesmen, the phrase is the "power of balance"— because only a salesman in balance can be truly successful. If you have the power of balance—and can keep your integrity, your discipline, your creativity, and your fearlessness—you have the way of the samurai!

Chapter 3: Self-Check Exercise
The Power of Balance

1. Explain how balancing the four pillars of success will help you become a samurai salesman in your current position.

    A. Integrity

    B. Discipline

    C. Creativity

    D. Fearlessness

2. Which of these pillars is the weakest in your life? What can you do to strengthen that pillar?

3. How does a high level of integrity help you sell more?

4. Explain how you can improve your performance through discipline. (Make certain you describe a system and not a program!)

5. Think creatively, "outside the box." Now, list three new ways to overcome a common sales obstacle you often face.

   1)

   2)

   3)

6. Where does fear keep you from being a samurai salesman?

7. How will you eliminate these fears and become fearless?

4

KEEP A

BEGINNER'S

MIND

THE PROBLEM WITH FINDING an *answer* is that it often marks the death of a *question*. If you are looking for "the answer" in sales techniques and think you have found it—forget it if you can, kill it if you can't. The only way to be a real master is to remain a student. Don't shut your mind down. Don't ever let your "routine" become routine. Don't become predictable. If you do, you are vulnerable and will start losing sales, because your competitors will know what you will do or say in any given situation. This is not to say you should not remain disciplined, that you shouldn't keep your tools sharp and your presentation polished, but don't become a slave to these things. Keep an open mind, be alert to change and chance, and be aware that opportunities, like problems, sometimes appear unexpectedly.

Sales is a changing game. Competition is getting stronger. Prospects are more demanding about the kind of products and services they want. The volume of information to be absorbed is constantly growing. Television used to be confined to three network stations in a market. Now cable routinely brings thirty to fifty offerings. We are approaching sensory overload.

A recent article in *Fortune* discussed experiments done on animals in which scientists progressively increased the sensory impressions given the test animals. As a result, the animals were soon unable to make even the simplest decision. Preliminary studies show that humans, too, are subject to sensory overload. When we get inundated with data, we decide *not* to decide.

Robert Ornstein, a leading neuroscientist, says that one mistake traditional brain researchers make is failing to consider the history of the human brain. If one goes back to the first appearance of human beings on this planet, our decisions were rather simple:

1. Get in the cave or stay in the rain.
2. Fight the animal or run.
3. Eat now or wait and see if something better comes along.

Our brain was designed to help us *survive* in a concrete, physical world we could see, hear, and feel. In fact, Orstein humorously sums up our ancient ancestors' concerns as "the four Fs—feeding, fighting, fleeing, and sexual reproduction!"

Considering the simplicity of our early decision-making and the complex decisions required of us today, an engineer might say that we humans are attempting to "exceed specifications." No wonder we spend so much on psychiatrists, prescriptions, placebos, and pity parties! We are a simple people living in a complex world. Worse than that, we live in a world that prides itself on its complexity. If a product has 150 features and 300 benefits, there are those who would teach you that you must share each and every one of them with your prospect. Try it, and you'll either beat your prospect to death, or he or she will beat a hasty retreat.

There's nothing intrinsically wrong with 150 features and 300 benefits. That's wonderful, if it's true. The problem is no one can assimilate that many. You have to investigate each prospect's "hot buttons" so that you can find out the few they will use to make their decision.

Even if we had the ability to process so many options, no one has the time. Today, to stay the same is to fall behind. Look at the Olympics. Just a few years ago, the person who did the triple axels in skating won the contest. Now everyone must do these just to make the competition. In the U.S. Olympic swim trials, the difference between first and twenty-fifth place in the 100-meter breastroke was 5.52 seconds! *A small difference in performance can make the difference between winning and losing an athletic event—or a sale!*

To stay on top means you have to be constantly alert to new and more effective techniques so you can incorporate them into your tool set. This state of alertness is the beginner's mind.

1. Keep an Empty Cup

A LESSON FROM THE ANCIENT SAMURAI

Years ago there was a story of a very learned warrior who visited a Zen monk and asked the monk to teach him the beginner's mind that every true samurai possesses. The monk said, "I will be happy to do this, but, first, perhaps you would like a cup of tea." Since it had been a long journey, the warrior agreed. The monk went off to make tea and returned with a teapot and a full cup of tea. He gave the full cup to the warrior and then began pouring in more tea. The hot tea went into the warrior's lap, badly burning him. "What are you doing?" the warrior cried, jumping to his feet. "The cup was already filled, and you kept pouring!"

The monk smiled. "That cup is a symbol of your mind. You came with a full cup. There was no place for anything new. You thought you knew it all, but the mind of the samurai is never full. It is always empty, always ready to receive something new."

2. *Always Stay Open to Learning*

What kind of salesperson are you? Do you congratulate yourself on all the sales you've made, books you've read, seminars you've attended? Are you proud of how much you know? Be careful, lest your mind become a filled cup, unable to hold anything more.

Would you feel comfortable going to a doctor who graduated from medical school at the top of her class forty years ago, but who was too lazy to keep up with new advances in medicine? Or would you rather go to a doctor who kept a beginner's mind, and who was always open, always questing, always learning?

A beginner's mind keeps you open for creative solutions. Let's look at how that mind-set can help create solutions.

Tale of a Modern Samurai

Sarah, a samurai, was in a sales situation where a major

prospect of hers was getting cold feet about selecting her company. They were concerned that they would not receive the type of service they needed, and this fear stalled the whole deal.

During a Corporate Visions training program on the Samurai Selling System, she saw a videotape about Lou Holtz, the coach of the Notre Dame football team, talking on how you should do right by the people around you. She knew the message on the tape was exactly what she wanted to tell her prospect. She set up a meeting and showed the tape to them, saying the message she wanted them to get was that she would do right by them, then listed examples of what she meant by "doing right." The prospect was so moved by her approach that they showed the tape to their entire staff during their next staff meeting, telling them that this was the way they should treat their own clients.

The result? Our samurai got her biggest sale of the year, her client got a great system, and the people her client served got better service. And it all came about because Sarah kept a beginner's mind.

As a side note, the prospect later told our samurai that seeing the tape was the conclusive factor in their decision! Isn't it interesting that a samurai-sense of service made everyone richer?

Lou's three rules are:

- Do what's right.
- Do the best you can.
- Treat others as you would like to be treated.

A THOUGHT FROM THE ANCIENT SAMURAI

"If you open your hand, you can take hold of anything. If you close your hand, nothing can enter it."
—Taisen Dewshimaru

3. Don't Get Locked into Technique

Samurai were taught that there were three elements that guided them to success: *shin*, or mind; *wasa*, or technique; and *tai*, or body. In a fight where one samurai had a strong body and the other a strong technique, they were convinced that technique would prevail. In a fight between a samurai with a strong technique and one with a strong mind, mind would prevail, because it would always find a weak point. We hear the same thing in the sports arena today.

Remember that all great artists have good technique, but great art requires more than mere technique. If you become attached to one selling technique, you are an aging warrior, a full cup, and you are less valuable than one who is constantly a student and refuses to get locked into a discipline. Great artists master technique, then transcend it; mediocre artists master technique and then become slaves to it! What kind of selling art will you practice?

Just a few years ago sales pros were taught formulas for selling like the Ben Franklin close, the open probe/closed probe, etc. Meanwhile, Dale Carnegie courses were teaching salespeople how to build a salesburger, sandwiching benefits between features and nailing it down with a clincher for a toothpick. These techniques have limited application in today's selling environment. If we become a slave to technique, we become has-beens in a world where the "new and improved" rule and reign.

The samurai who became "too good" to practice, "too set in his ways" to seek new techniques, was a liability to those he served. No one knowingly employs a warrior who will lose in battle. No company wants a salesperson who will consistently come in second against the competition. A company spends its time and money on salespeople who come in first—and that means the person who keeps a beginner's mind.

The beginner's mind is the mind of a child. Ever watch a child when you put a bright, new toy within reach? He or she is entranced, enthralled, excited, and anxious to explore it. The trick to success in sales is never to lose that childlike mind-set. This is much more difficult to do than to say, because as we "mature," we sometimes become jaded. We begin to think we've seen and heard it all before. Pretty soon we find a technique, a tool, a teaching, and we use it over and over, applying it almost by rote as though we were in the two thousandth performance of a badly scripted play. We are going through the motions, with no fresh ideas. Someone mentions "sales training," and we go, "Ugh! I've done that. I know all that stuff. I was doing that when you were learning your ABCs." When someone says (or thinks) that, he's trying to say, "I know all I need to know." What they're really saying is, "My cup is already full."

If you earn your living through sales, you must never lose the beginner's mind. You must be the master of all you compete against. You must have great techniques, solid discipline and a strong *ki*.

Your "enemy" is your competitor, and your competitor has probably learned to defend him- or herself against all your ancient wiles. If you are not continually learning new techniques and tools, then you may find yourself slipping into second place in a profession where there are no second-place winners.

A beginner's mind is always young and alive. It is always searching. It uses what it knows and is always open to the new. Keep the beginner's mind, and your skills will stay so sharp that your keenest competition is not your competitor, but yourself. The hard part won't be making the quota your company gives you, but making the quota you set for yourself. Funny thing, a beginner's mind is hardly ever discovered in an average salesperson. It's always found in top sales professionals!

In our seminars we often find that those who are most interested and most turned on are the top producers. They are like sponges, actively listening and learning, seeking one new skill or idea that they can incorporate into their selling skills.

At one seminar we taught, we got an evaluation from one attendee that read, "I didn't learn anything new in your course." This really concerned us, because we take pride in presenting new and valuable sales concepts. When we checked, we found this particular salesperson performed in the bottom fourth of his company. He was saying, "My cup is already full, and I don't need any more tea!" We might have thought his evaluation correct had it not been for the others we received from the same group. One read, "I have taken numerous sales courses, read many books, have built a tape and video library on selling. I have had the highest sales in my company for the last five years. Yours is the best training experience I have had to date and the only one that puts the whole commitment process together." Had the top producer heard any of these things before? Yes, many of them. Yet top performers are alert to new concepts or even a new shading on something they have already learned, because they realize that subtle shad-ings can make the difference between success and fail-ure.

A LESSON FROM THE SAMURAI

In *Lives of Master Swordsmen*,[9] Makoto Sugawara relates how a man learning the way of the samurai began with a beginner's mind. In effect, he says, "As one progresses from the beginner stage through the different levels of training, he reaches such a state of knowledge that one realizes he will always be a beginner! For example, during the beginner stage a person knows nothing about the proper manner of holding a sword. So if he is attacked, he seizes the sword and defends himself without calculation. As he progresses beyond the beginner stage, he studies various techniques, and his knowledge increases. Yet, if he is attacked, he is likely to hesitate while trying to decide which method of defense to use. Eventually he progresses to the point where he can master sword and technique almost without thought. His choice of technique comes as naturally as breathing to him. At this point, his state of mind is as free as it was when he was a beginner—though he has the skill of a master."

The point made is a good one. There is much to be gained by learning all the techniques of selling, but they don't really come into play unless you retain a begin-

9. Sugawara, *Master Swordsmen*, p. 222. Adapted by permis-sion.

ner's mind. Tactics adhered to slavishly in the face of changing circumstances inevitably result in defeat, as our next samurai story illustrates.

Li Ching was Chinese and so not officially a samurai, but the soul of the samurai lived within him because he had a beginner's mind. When he was sent to capture the rebel Hsien in 621, he was stopped by the annual flooding of the Yangtze river. His generals urged him to wait until the water had receded and the river was safer to navigate. But Li Ching knew that advice came from the mind of a master and not a beginner. Down the river, Hsien would be trying to think with the mind of an expert and would have come to the same conclusion—that they could never attack down the river. So, thinking with a beginner's mind, he realized that this was the very route his attack must take! Hsien's army was surprised, and Li Ching's forces were victorious.

One way to cultivate a beginner's mind is to play an active role in your development. Don't wait for your organization to hire a sales coach; take charge of your own destiny. Constantly absorb sales tapes. Keep reading books about the profession and attend any seminars that seem worthwhile. Don't accept all you see and hear uncritically. Each time you get an idea, ask yourself, "Will that work?" If the answer is yes, then ask yourself, "How will I use it?"

*   *   *

4. Be the Prospect

It's easier to keep a beginner's mind if you keep looking at the world through your prospect's eyes. See what he sees. Feel what he feels. What emotions, joys, pleasures, and pains is he feeling? Get inside his business and learn what life is like for him during a typical business day. As you do this, you will begin to get ideas about how to serve him. This is a beginner's mind.

We remember reading that an eleven-foot-tall truck got wedged under a ten-foot, ten-inch overpass. Adults on the scene were prying the metal back on the truck cab to free the vehicle. A child stood watching a minute, then went up to one of the workers and said, "Mister, if that were my truck, I wouldn't want it torn up this way. I'd just let some air out of the tires and push it back!" A beginner's mind at work had found an elegant solution.

When you have a beginner's mind and are completely able to become part of the prospect's world, you will have no problem in figuring out how to use a new concept. Whenever you're stymied or stumped, just switch on your beginner's mind, and solutions will come to you.

A Modern Samurai Story

Sam was a sales samurai who sold information systems for a living. For some time he had been working with a certain client trying to convince her to invest $2 million for a limited installation of the system. The sales process was proceeding smoothly. There had been numerous presentations, site visits, demos, and even justification reports written and approved. Suddenly the prospect's executive vice president called a halt to the procedure.

Recognizing that delay is fatal to a sale, Sam reviewed all that had happened, trying to keep a beginner's mind. He realized suddenly that the executive VP was a "get-involved" type of person who would rather be doing than listening. So he

asked him for fifteen minutes to show him a part of the demo.
When the VP arrived, instead of showing him the demo, Sam
got him to sit at the terminal and play with the system him-
self. The VP was so excited, he asked to be given a full run-
down that afternoon. Then the VP gave the demonstration to
the board of directors—by himself! The board was also excited
and offered to authorize the $2 million limited installation.
The VP surprised them with this response, "We don't need a
$2 million project. We need to approve $23 million so we can
install the system in company headquarters next year and
allocate an additional $75 million to phase it in companywide
over the next five years!"

The samurai would never have won this huge sale if he
had blindly followed a sales "technique" manual. It
took the fresh thinking of the beginner's mind to do the
job.

To be a samurai, in ancient or modern times, we must
remain open to new things, always wondering if something will work, and if so, how we can make it work for
us. A true samurai is always a student.

A samurai saying goes, "There is no need to wonder
where the arrow is going to land." The arrow will go
where the mind and hand of the samurai send it, so
once it is released, he can turn his attention to other
things. This is one reason samurai selling is so exhilarat-
ing—because practiced skills, coupled with a beginner's
mind, enables each contest to be approached with fresh
enthusiasm. By contrast, ordinary salespeople tire
quickly of the conflict and invariably fall to the superior
way of the samurai salesman.

Chapter 4:
Self-Check Quiz

1. In your own words write the moral of the fable about the monk who poured the would-be samurai a "full cup of tea."

2. In our training seminars we usually find that top performers are more open to new ideas than poor performers. Why do you think that is true?

3. What does it mean to have a "beginner's mind"?

4. Think of a sales obstacle you have had to closing business (price too high, sales deferrals, etc.). Now use a beginner's mind and create a totally new solution!

5. Just for a moment, let all preconceived notions and ideas drain from your mind like water from a basin. Now, think about your most challenging prospect, and put your beginner's mind to work on ways you might move toward a close. In the space below, write down some of the ideas that come to you.

5

CREATING

A SENSE

OF URGENCY

IT IS POSSIBLE, OF COURSE, to do everything described in the first four chapters of this book and to fail as a samurai if you don't create a sense of buying urgency in your prospect. Samurai referred to this sense of urgency as "living as if a fire were raging in your hair."

That is a very colorful metaphor, isn't it? What would your prospect do if his hair were on fire? Sit around and discuss whether this called for a type A, B, or C fire extinguisher? Debate whether to douse it with water or to try wrapping it in a towel? Dispassionately discuss the merits of calling the fire department directly relative to dialing 911? We think he'd be begging you to put it out as quickly as possible using whatever means were at hand!

How do you set his hair on fire? By creating strong emotions! When we feel a strong emotion, our bodies release several hormones into our system. A recent study shows that hungry laboratory rats had an easier time finding food at the end of a maze when they were injected with a "hormonal cocktail" consisting of all the naturally occurring, stress-related hormones created by emotions. The rats didn't become hungrier or smarter, but their senses were excited, so they made decisions faster. When you get your prospect to thinking about his problem, he gets to feeling the stress. The next thing he knows, his hair is on fire and he wants instant relief! An excited prospect just naturally begins to move more quickly toward the prize at the end of the maze.

A sense of urgency is contagious. Prospects catch it from you. When the prospect begins to feel a sense of urgency, he or she wants to act immediately. We may look at a provider or service if we think we *need* it, but the whole process gains momentum when it's something we *want*! We buy from emotion, from want. That's where a good samurai earns his or her keep. A good samurai salesman creates urgency through the heart, through the emotions…and plays on those emotions the way Isaac Stern plays a violin.

Urgency is an emotional commitment. It allows the samurai salesman and the prospect to reach objectives quickly, because each wants to get the product, or system or service in place ASAP so that it can begin solving the prospect's problem. You *want* to solve them; you *need* to solve them; you want and need to solve them *now!*

When there's a sense of urgency, the sale moves along quickly and steadily; more important, obstacles move out of the way. The sale has energy and momentum. It is every salesperson's dream deal. Here's the rub: Without urgency, you don't even have a qualified prospect!

HOW IMPORTANT IS URGENCY TO YOU?

The best way to create urgency in others is first to create it in yourself. A good way to develop a sense of urgency is to ask yourself, "How much money would I earn if I closed all the accounts now 'pending'?" Let's pause a moment while you ask yourself that question.

Well, how much money do you have at stake? Only you know the answer, but we're betting that there's a lot of money waiting to be harvested. Does thinking about it create butterflies in your stomach? Do you feel yourself getting "antsy" to get on with this chapter and get the other skills you need to become a true samurai salesman? Are you already counting the customers you can close, the money you can make, the things you can do? Congratulations! You're developing a sense of urgency!

In this chapter we aren't going to show you how to "push" your prospect toward a decision. Instead, we're going to show you how to get the prospect to "pull" you through the sales process. In fact, your prospect will get so fired up, he or she will become your "inside sales force." The prospect will be supplying *you* with the energy for the sale instead of the other way around!

The urgency we're talking about is *genuine* urgency, not "discount" urgency. "Buy it today because it either (a) goes off sale tomorrow or (b) goes up tomorrow" isn't real urgency. The only motivation produced by "discount" urgency is that of saving a dollar, and prospects won't be willing to do that unless you've first created an urgency to have their problems solved!

CREATING GENUINE URGENCY

What are the steps needed to create *genuine* urgency? There are four:

1. Be one with the buyer.
2. Speak simply.
3. Sell to the subconscious mind.
4. Remember the power of questions.

1. Be One with the Buyer

In order to serve your prospect, you must become one with them. You must see as they see, hear as they hear, feel as they feel. Look through their eyes. What do they see? How do their lives, their jobs, their careers seem to them? Listen with their ears. How do you sound to them? What are the people *they* serve saying? What do they *want* to hear and why? Feel what they are feeling. Feel their problems, feel their pain, ask them about it. What upsets them? Are the upsets so painful that they demand solutions now?

Each person lives in his own private universe. In order to serve, a samurai salesman must share the universe of his prospect. The samurai's focus must be entirely on the prospect, finding ways to bring him the things he wants. When you come to believe this, your prospect will sense it and begin to believe it, too. Your whole attitude will be saying, "I am here to help. We will work together."

The prospect is pushing a wheelbarrow filled with hopes, cares, fears, and dreams. So are you. Do not dump your load of features on him, but help him carry his load of problems. Consider this carefully: *His problems must be heavier than your products, or he will never trade them in!*

Help, but do not do all the work for the prospect. Get commitments. Get her involved. If many steps must be completed before the sale is closed, get her to commit to do something early with a "by when" date. Work as a partnership with each of you doing your share. You are there to be of service—not to be merely a servant.

In your effort to be one with the buyer, you must gather more information than you give, because you must know where it hurts in order to make it better. You must know where that prospect wants to be with that new car, new house, new stereo, new TV, new investment. Otherwise, you can not help him arrive at his destination.

2. Speak Simply

Talk as they talk, using language they understand. If they speak like generals, of strategy, then talk strategic concepts. If they speak like soldiers, of tactics, then focus on tactical solutions. Success comes to the samurai who can make complex things sound exciting and dull things sound interesting.

As you speak, use stories, metaphors, and analogies to make your message easier to understand and remember. A story is more powerful than a fact, because a story involves the imagination and the subconscious mind.

When Lincoln was bothered by people trying to influence him, he told a story of a farmer who lost his way one dark night in a thunderstorm. Lincoln said, "The peals of thunder were terrific...the earth seemed to tremble beneath him. One bolt threw him to his knees. Finding himself in this position, he decided to pray. 'Oh God! Hear my prayer at this time, for Thou knowest it isn't often I call on Thee. And O Lord! If it's all the same to Thee, give us a little more light and a little less noise'" By using an amusing story, Lincoln was able to make his point in just a few words.

Mark Twain, never at a loss for words, used a humorous story to convince preachers of the danger of long sermons. He wrote, "Some years ago in Hartford, we all went to church one hot sweltering night to hear the annual report of Mr. Hawley, a city missionary who went around finding people who needed help and didn't want to ask for it. He told of the life in cellars, where poverty resided; he gave instances of the heroism and devotion of the poor. 'When a man with millions gives,' he said, 'we make a great deal of noise. It is noise in the wrong place, for it's the widow's might that counts.' Well, Hawley worked me up to a great pitch. I could hardly wait for him to get through. I had $400 in my pocket, I wanted to give that and borrow more to give. You could see greenbacks in every eye. But instead of passing the plate then, he kept on talking and talking, and as he talked it grew hotter and hotter, and we grew sleepier and sleepier. My enthusiasm went down, down down—$100 at a clip—until finally, when the plate did come around, I stole ten cents out of it just to spite him for keeping me so long."

The two stories we just shared not only served the original authors' purposes, but serve to remind us today to give "a little more light and a little less noise" and to speak concisely so we do not lose our audience.

When you tell a story, tell it simply, in few words, but with powerful visual images. Make the message and benefit easy to remember, so it can be a rallying point for the prospect and the people he or she must influence!

3. Sell to the Subconscious Mind

The prospect can see things in his mind's eye that don't exist in the physical world. He can feel what is not there by thinking about how it would feel. This is a tremendous power we possess. Harness it in your selling!

Once you find the prospect's problems, create the pain in his mind. He feels the pain subconsciously. It hurts. He burns for a solution. Introduce your product or service as something that can take the pain away. Get him to buy your product mentally, use it, feel the joy of it.

The subconscious mind can feel joy as well as pain. In order for your buyer to subconsciously use your product, he has to first mentally own it. You have just jumped over the close, when he is already using it! Help him visualize the result he wants! Make it a happy time!

Create in your prospect's mind the image you want through stories, visualization, and focusing on both the dreary past before the product and the pleasant future with the product.

4. Remember the Power of Questions

To keep the product or service working in his mind, use the power of questions. Think more about the questions you will ask than you do about the answers you will give. A prospect may listen passively when you talk, but questions demand involvement. The right questions engage his intellect and emotions.

Question with integrity, question innocently, but question relentlessly. Most salespeople ask too few questions, and those they do ask are often of little value. Plan your questions in advance, knowing questions are your ultimate sales tools. Use them to help you find better ways to serve your prospect and to help him better realize how he needs to be served. Remember, if you don't like the results you are getting, ask better questions!

Realize that each reply is like the tip of an iceberg—there is more hidden than revealed. Ask follow-up questions to discover what was behind the reply. Probe, but do not interrogate. Question as though you were walking on rice paper and wanted to leave no damage. Move with his spirit instead of against it, and he will rightly perceive your motive in asking as a desire to serve.

Do not merely ask questions to find out facts, but to uncover feelings. Facts are dry as tinder, but feelings are hot sparks that ignite emotions. If you are selling automobiles and the prospect needs a dependable automobile, that is a fact. Find out how he will use this automobile and you uncover the feelings about family and power and prestige. These sparks ignite the facts and create a fire that you can fan to full force.

Sometimes you need to tape-record your conversation and play it back later. How much time did you spend talking about you and your products and services, and how much time did you spend asking about his problems and how they are affecting him? Remember, *selling is not about you, it is about him.* Involve your prospect in the search for solutions, and he'll set his own hair on fire!

GOING APE

Learning the art of masterful questioning is like a samurai keeping his sword sharp. Let's explore a form of questioning that will create buying urgency. In our seminars, we refer to it as "going APE." No, we aren't switching from samurai to simian analogies! We use "APE" as an acronym for the three types of questions samurai salesmen ask to create a sense of urgency.

Samurai go APE for three reasons. First, they use APE questions to find out if an account is really qualified. Second, they use APE questions to uncover problems and build a sense of urgency. Third, they use APE questions to get the effect they want.

APE = Account + Problem + Effect

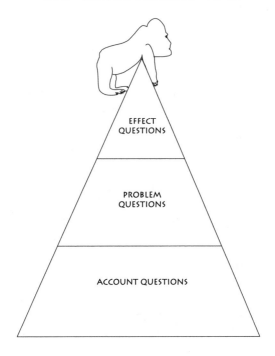

EFFECT
QUESTIONS

PROBLEM
QUESTIONS

ACCOUNT QUESTIONS

"A" is for **Account** questions. The first thing you've got to do in qualifying the account is to make sure they are the right kind of account for your product or service.

Account questions are those that find out the physical attributes of the account or prospect. Who is looking for this product? Who will use it? Who will make the decision? You need to know this just to determine if you're right for one another, and if you are, to discover with whom you should be talking.

All salespeople ask account questions. Samurai salespeople ask *excellent* account questions. They ask questions that are specific, comprehensive, and honest in order to determine if the product or service makes sense for the prospect. If so, they play on. If not, why play the game if no one can win?

"P" is for **Problem** questions. If we don't have problems to solve, then we don't have jobs, do we? How do we find out what problems the prospect faces? We ask. Prospects have told us that, as a rule, salespeople ask lousy questions. As one home buyer remarked, "It's almost as if the realtors are afraid to ask me about my life and lifestyle!"

Just about every salesperson will *eventually* ask diagnostic questions that reveal problems, but samurai salesmen ask those questions early in the procedure, so they can tailor every word, every move, every fact to solving those problems.

Proper, problem-finding questions get answers like:

- "I need a new car with 4-wheel drive because. . . ."
  "I'm thinking of a room addition because I like this house and it's cheaper to remodel than it is to move."
- "I was thinking of siding my house because. . . ."
- "We can't keep orders straight with our existing computer."
- "We're getting behind in production."

Two things happen when we ask problem-finding questions and listen to the answers. First, as samurai salespeople, we get a handle on how we can help. Secondly, as the prospect begins to talk about the problems, he finds himself getting involved, which is the first step in creating a *sense of urgency.*

"E" is for **Effect** questions. Problems don't hurt. The *effects* of the problems are what hurt. If you have a hole in your tooth, that's a problem. So? So, left alone, the effect will be that the tooth will begin to hurt! You have a problem when you put your hand on a hot stove. It's the effect of this that makes you more aware of the problem!

Unhappy customers are a problem. The effects are *lost customers*, lost revenue, lost income, lost jobs. Thinking about the effect causes one to feel the pain. Any pain gets worse the more you think about it and talk about it. When prospects begin telling you where it hurts, they remember their pain and they want something done now!

Through questioning, you are trying to get the prospect to feel the heat—and set his hair on fire. That is the sense of urgency we're wanting to create. So, encourage them to talk about their problems and specifically how those problems affect them. Don't be afraid to ask effect questions such as "What effect does that problem have here in your company?" "What happens when this occurs?" and "How are you affected? What is the impact on other people here?" Remember, effect questions that focus on the impact of unsolved problems will create excitement in your sales!

Most ordinary salespeople never get to the effect questions. As soon as the prospect explains the problem, they leap in and pitch the product or service immedi-ately. A superior salesman explains the value of his product or service only after he learns about the effects. Our samurai waits even longer, biding her time—*and fanning the flames*! She is a persistent questioner and a sympathetic listener. Once the prospect senses your sincere desire to help and sees that you feel the pain with him, he will become open to the solutions you offer.

This is where urgency pays off. The pain of the effects hurts him personally, and he wants to do something about it immediately, if not sooner. (As one prospect semifacetiously groaned, "This isn't just a matter of life and death. *It's much more important than that!*") Now the samurai can really begin to work on solving the prospect's problems, because the prospect is anxious to have them solved!

Bed of the Samurai

Recently Chuck decided to purchase a new box spring and mattress. In the first store, he found a bed that was comfortable and was marked down from $900 to $500. The salesman replied, "This is a good bed for the price." When asked about the competitive advantage, he said, "All mattresses are basically the same. Some wire the coils east to west, others north to south. Just don't buy the ones that are independently wired, because they can eventually pop out of their cloth pockets. The way to buy a mattress is to lie on it, and if it feels good and the price is right, buy it."

At the second store, they sold the type of independently wired mattress the first salesman had warned about. The salesman asked, "Are you looking for a mattress for yourself?" (Account question.) He then asked, "Are you getting rid of an older mattress?" (Another Account question.) Upon receiving an affirmative reply, he asked, "Was it not working well for you?" (Problem question.) "Why were you unhappy with it?"(Effect question.) With these questions, the salesman learned that a perfectly good waterbed was being replaced because Chuck woke up with a sore back too often. Understanding the problem, he asked Chuck, "How do you sleep, on your side, back, or stomach?" (Account question.) He then inquired where Chuck's back hurt. (Effect question.)

After those questions it was obvious that the salesman both understood and sympathized with the problem. Chuck says, "My back was beginning to hurt just thinking about it! The salesman gave a convincing reason why I was bothered with the waterbed. He went on to tell me why a standard mattress, where the springs are wired together, wouldn't do either. He said, 'We sell them, but they're not for you.' He then demonstrated what he meant with a prop shaped like a torso. He showed how ordinary mattresses create tension on the back, compressing the vertebrae and creating more pain. (Effect.)"

Chuck said the salesman then took the torso tool and showed what happened on the individually wired springs, showing how each spring supported the back and told how

*this would improve Chuck's back problem. (Effect of the sales-
man's solution.)*

Now, which mattress do you think Chuck bought,
the $500 mattress where the coils were wired together or
the $1399 one where the coils were wired indepen-
dently? *The one the samurai sold, of course!* Chuck says,
"By the time he finished with me, my back was hurting
so badly, I made him promise to deliver it the next day!"
(Yes, it's very comfortable, and Chuck's back is much
better, thank you.)

The moral is that even a samurai salesman is an
easy mark for another samurai salesman. The business
went to the salesman who uncovered the underlying
reason for the product search. He was able to create a
consultative position for himself and, through the use of
good product demos and effect questions, to close the
sale—*for almost three times the price of the other product!*

Scientists are learning that while different parts of
our brain control specific behaviors, all sections of the
brain "check in" with the part that governs our emotions before making a buying decision. So while we may
give facts as the reason for our decision, reasons apparently don't count unless they relate to our emotions!

When you're discussing the pain, remember that
individuals, not organizations, make decisions. So while
the pain the organization feels is important, the pain of
the prospect is even more important. The true samurai
taps into that pain and fans it into a fire of urgency.

Why Do Salespeople Have Trouble Creating Urgency?

A sense of urgency follows a samurai as surely as dawn
follows midnight. Yet some salespeople say that they
have a hard time creating a sense of urgency in their
accounts. When we examine the reasons for their failure, we often find they do not fully believe in the prod-

uct they are selling or the company they are represent-ing. (If this is your problem, either change companies, or go back and reread Chapter 2, and work on your *ki!*) Other times, there is simply no burning issue the sales-person can solve for the prospect, but he dutifully keeps trying. When a samurai senses that there is no urgency and he is unable to create urgency, he moves on, because one who is committed to service must have someone to serve.

A samurai doesn't have time to fight unwinnable battles. If he cannot quickly create a sense of urgency, he or she drops the prospect and moves on to another account. If you keep on trying to win an unwinnable account, you're only hurting yourself because the ac-count will begin to feel pushed or pressured. We are reminded of the homespun homily, "Never try to teach a pig to sing. You can't do it, and it just frustrates the pig!" You not only are wasting your time on this account, but you are *not* spending time on another account you could win—if you were there.

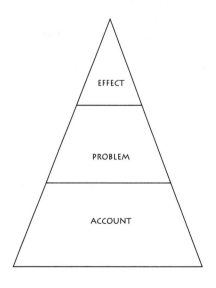

Keep in mind that you only have a qualified prospect when he feels the effects of his problems and his hurt! Run through the APE triangle and only sell at the top! Remember the advice given by the world-famous fisherman, "Fish where the fish are." You waste too much of your time if you try to sell the entire APE triangle. When you create a sense of urgency in the effect stage, the prospect will *pull you into the account!* He will become a salesperson for you. That's a qualified account!

The Real Power of Urgency

By using problem-effect questions, you develop an understanding of the true passion associated with the prospect's problem areas. If you introduce your products and/or services as solutions to those problems, the prospect is all ears—eager to learn, and actively thinking about how your solutions will help. Now, as you introduce your solution, be sure to discuss the effect your solution will bring, not just the features. Once you've established how your solution fits his situation, turn to effect questions again. Ask the prospect to share with you how he sees your solution helping them. When he begins to share those insights with you, he will mentally begin using your product, begin to feel the joy of using it, and become excited by it. In effect, the prospect is now selling you!

The Samurai Agent

Recently, during one of our sales training seminars, a salesman told us how an insurance agent sold him a policy. The agent arrived after work and talked to him and his wife. First, the agent gathered the necessary account information (name, age, place of work, income, wife's age, work, dependents, etc.). Next, the agent asked problem-related questions. How much money did it take to keep the household afloat in case of the husband's death; how much money would be needed for the children's education; and similar questions. Then he asked permission to play a short video that discussed the effects on the household when the sole provider leaves the family unprotected. In the video the happy family went through the tragic death of husband and father. He had no insurance, their small savings were soon consumed, and the bills piled up until they were forced to sell the house.

When the video was over, the agent asked, "If—heaven forbid—something should happen to you, think of how your family would be affected! Think how much better they would fare if you had this policy!"

The salesman told our group, "I looked at my wife and saw tears running down her face! How could I have refused to buy the policy? I would have seemed insensitive and uncaring!"

Living with a Sense of Urgency

Want to get ahead? First, create a sense of urgency in yourself! Write down on a piece of paper the sales goals you have for this year. Next, ask yourself an effect question: What will happen if I don't reach that goal? List all the effects of failure. Itemize the pain, the frustration, the fear, the damage to your ego and sense of self-worth. Then, begin to create solutions for achieving your goals. Move from the *pain* to the *pleasure* you'll receive when you make your new quota. Think of all the effects of reaching your sales goal. Think of the additional revenues, the financial freedom, and the things you will do with the money. Now think of the additional power you'll have where you work, how much easier it will be for you to get things done. Think of how it will help your career. As you begin to do that, you will begin to get more excited about reaching that goal. This is what feeling a sense of urgency is all about!

Now, really paint yourself in a corner. Go public with your commitment of what you'll produce this year. Write it down; send it to your boss; hang it up on your wall. Okay, now get to work. You have a lot to do, but you'll have a ball doing it!

Chapter 5: Self-Check Quiz

1. What is "buying urgency?"

2. How will you create a sense of urgency in yourself?

3. How can you create a sense of urgency in your prospects?

4. What is "APE"?

5. Now, let's put APE to work for you! Think about a prospect you lost. Now fill in what you know about them:

      Account information:

      Problem information:

Effects of these problems on the decision maker:

6. For a prospect you just won, fill in the same information:

Account information:

Problem information:

Effects of these problems on the decision maker:

7. Think of a top prospect you have. What effect questions do you want to ask?

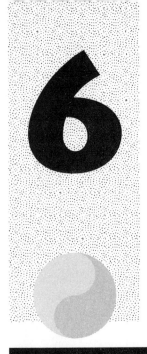

6

THE

COMPETITIVE

SAMURAI

Lou Capps—Modern Samurai

Lou Capps is a master salesman. When he was a boy of eight, he was making and selling trinkets to mothers in his neighborhood and slingshots to their kids. As he grew older, he worked at a variety of selling jobs and, quite naturally, made sales his career. In his forties he became one of the highest-paid salespeople in his company and frequently doubled or even tripled his quota.

Few things bring more joy to a parent than being a positive role model and mentor for his or her children. Lou was pleased when his youngest daughter, Sheila (whom you met in the first chapter), also chose a sales career. Ably trained by her samurai father, Sheila quickly became one of the most successful salespeople in her firm. She regularly exceeded quota and had a long list of happy customers. Lou was surprised then when Sheila called and said she wondered if she belonged in selling at all. "Why would you think that?" Lou asked.

"Dad, I lost this account I've been working on for months, and I'm really demoralized. I feel so low, I could sit on a wet Kleenex and swing my legs! I worked hard on the deal, used all the techniques you taught me, got close to them, and knew what problems they are facing. I can stand losing— barely," she added quickly, "but our solutions were not only the best solutions, but the issues on which they based their decision weren't particularly important. I'm doubly upset. One reason is that I lost. The other reason is that I'm convinced they lost, too!"

Lou listened intently as Sheila ran through the details of the sale and its subsequent loss. He was pleased that she had learned to take personal responsibility for losing the sale and was willing to admit, albeit reluctantly, that she had been outsold.

When Sheila finished, Lou said, "Sheila, you have learned a valuable lesson in sales today. The one with the best solution doesn't always win. The one with the highest sense of service doesn't always win, either. Solutions and service are prerequisites for success, but the one who wins is not necessarily the best person with the best product but simply the best competitor!"

"I thought if I were the best at everything, I wouldn't have to worry about the competition!" Sheila lamented.

Lou chuckled. "Remember when I used to read you the story of The Tortoise and the Hare? *That's just what the hare thought, and he got complacent. Many a samurai soldier and thousands of samurai salesmen have lost because they underestimated the competition!"*

"I've always sort of pretended around my clients that the competition doesn't exist. I was afraid that the client might think I was engaging in negative selling if I pointed out the problems with their products. Don't you agree that it's unseemly for a samurai to engage in negative selling?"

"It's possible to sell competitively without selling nega-
tively," Lou reminded her. "Why don't you come over to the
house? I'll put on a pot of coffee and share some of the secrets
of superstar samurai."

"I'm sorry, Dad," she said, sighing. "Right now, all I can
concentrate on is losing this account! I don't know what I'm
going to tell them at the office tomorrow."

"A true samurai never panics, blaming product or price.
That's the mark of a real samurai! You may have outsold the
competition in the issues that were most important, but they
obviously outsold you in the issues that the prospect thought
were most important. You were outfoxed and—"

"And the fox ran away with the prize!" Sheila finished,
recalling a nursery story her father used to tell her.

"Not necessarily," Lou replied. "You may find you
haven't lost the account at all, but we'll get into that after I
share with you some samurai secrets on competitive selling—
and some of your Mom's famous blueberry cheesecake!"

"It's a deal, Dad," Sheila sighed, "but I don't see how
you can say that I may not have lost the account. They've
already announced—"

"As Yogi Berra said, 'It ain't over till it's over.' You
haven't tried all the weapons in your armory, and as Musashi
said, 'You must make fullest use of your weaponry. It is
false not to do so or to die with a weapon yet undrawn.'"

"What weapon haven't I drawn?"

"We'll get to that. Now you concentrate on getting your
ki right and on your driving and get over here! I've got a
strong feeling you can go back in there and snatch victory
from the jaws of defeat!"

A SUPER-SAMURAI'S
COMPETITIVE SELLING SECRETS

Boiled down, these are the super-samurai's competitive
selling secrets Lou shared with Sheila when she arrived

that evening. (We're only sorry we couldn't include a sample of the blueberry cheesecake!)

1. Know Your Competitor

In Chapter 2, we wrote about the importance of knowing yourself. That is the first rule of being a samurai. The first rule of competition is to get to know your competitor. Sun Tsu wrote, "If you know the enemy and know yourself, you need not fear the result of a hundred battles. If you know yourself but not the enemy, for every victory gained, you will also suffer a defeat. If you know neither the enemy nor yourself, you will succumb in every battle."

Knowledge of your competitors includes knowledge of their companies, their products, and their service. Where are they weak? Where are they strong? Where are they most likely to attack your product, service, or company? Where are they most vulnerable? Next, you must know the salesperson who is competing with you for the sale. There is often more difference between salespeople in the same company than there is between companies. You must know how your personal adversary is likely to act and react.

Where do you gain information about your competitors? Begin by studying their annual report and sales and technical literature. Interview existing clients and, if possible, obtain copies of old proposals. These are good for providing background information, but your best source of information about competitors is your prospect! Often, without realizing it, your prospect will tell you how your enemies are attacking and even give you glimpses of their battle strategy.

You will get a lot of information about your competitor indirectly from the prospect. Listen to the questions your prospect is asking and to the objections they are raising. Do they sound genuine, or do they sound like worries planted by your competitor? Whether the questions grew from genuine doubts or doubts planted by your competitor, how you respond to questions and objections is important. Never get flustered. Remember, these are the ways a prospect says, "Tell me more, I'm not certain I understand this!" Keep a beginner's mind. Never be defensive when responding, and by all means, never be offensive! Objections are often emotional, and as illogical as it seems, buying decisions are based on emotions and not just on fact.

Take a tip from the martial art of aikido, and gently guide your prospect to where *you* want him to be! The essence of aikido is that even in conflict, you not only protect yourself from harm, but your opponent as well! You don't confront or challenge the prospect's initial direction, you simply alter it. Chances are, she's heading in the direction where your competitor sent her. A clever competitor will have a prospect take you down a certain path so he can ambush you. As you guide your prospect back onto the proper path, you not only have rescued the sale, but you protected your prospect from harm! As a bonus, you have learned your competitor's game plan! Sun Tsu said, *"The sudden rising of birds in their flight is the sign of an ambush at the spot below."* When you see your prospect rise in fright at one point, you know where your enemy is hidden.

2. Pick the Issues

In the real world of modern business, there will be a competitive battle for each sale. You can't alter that, but you can pick the battleground! Like a good samurai, you will, of course, choose a battleground that puts you at an advantage and your competition at a disadvantage. In addition, you'll arrange obstacles, hindrances, and surprises for the competition while keeping your own movements cloaked in secrecy, like a stealthy samjurai. **If you can control the issues, you will control the sale.** Pick the issues that give you a competitive advantage and create an emotional reaction in the prospect.

No matter how long the laundry list of issues a prospect-company *says* are important, individuals make decisions based on issues that are important to *them*. So the hinges that cause the door to the sale to open will be based on a couple of hot, emotional issues that can blaze into a bonfire of buying. That's just the way the human mind works. This is true whether the prospect is buying a pen, an automobile, a life-insurance policy or a multi-million dollar computer system. Of course, the sale doesn't begin that way. The initial list you'll receive may contain dozens or even hundreds of issues. To move to the semifinals, each competitor has a product or service that reasonably satisfies those issues—that's a given. Once it's given, however, that list basically disappears and is replaced by one or two "hot issues" in the mind of the person or persons making the buying decision.

A dramatic example of this came to our attention recently. After a seven-month sales effort, the prospect picked Vendor A to deliver their accounting system services. Vendor B was dropped because they lacked much of Vendor A's functionality and were slightly more expensive. You can imagine how surprised Vendor A's salesman was when, at the last moment, he was informed that the prospect had changed his mind and decided to take Vendor B's system. Why? Because in Vendor A's accounting package, they calculated payroll checks to the nearest tenth of an hour, i.e., 6 minutes, 12 minutes, 18 minutes. However, the company was a union shop, and in the union agreement the employees pay was calculated to the nearest 15-minute interval. Under Vendor A's package, this meant that they would be underpaid by 3 minutes on certain days or overpaid by 3 minutes. The union, of course, voted to be overpaid. The company was fairly small, only a couple of hundred employees, so this overpayment amounted to only a few hundred dollars a year. Small change, considering the cost of the entire product, and it was thousands of dollars less than the difference between Vendor A's price and Vendor B's price. The kicker was that the owner of the company hated the union and would rather have been skinned alive than give the union an extra penny over what was in the contract. He felt so strongly about this that he paid Vendor B a higher price for an inferior product! It was the *emotion* of the decision maker that made the difference!

Sounds illogical, doesn't it? It is. However, the world does not always run on logic. Sometimes emotion is the deciding factor.

Recently a top U.S. university bought over $500,000 worth of specialized equipment. When we interviewed them and asked why they chose that product over competitive offerings, they replied, "We just liked their people better!" In other words, they made a $500,000 emotional decision!

Often we find that people would rather have one, good, honest emotion in making a decision than a hundred facts. In our own collective experience, we have seen prospect after prospect downplay facts and decide on emotion. Some have even made long laundry lists of issues and assigned point values for each. They'd add them up and call in the top two or three ranking vendors. Then they'd ignore all that and make a decision based on a couple of emotional issues on their personal agendas, which may or may not have been on the original list!

Since this is true, knowing what those couple of emotional issues are is vital to your success. The best way to make certain that you know what these issues are is to help the prospect and/or the prospect group in selecting them. Get there early and be part of the battle plan!

SELL TO INDIVIDUALS, NOT TO A GROUP

When you are facing an account where several people are involved in the decision making, it is natural to attempt to present to them as a group. This is a common practice. Unfortunately, it is also a common mistake. Groups aren't homogeneous. They are composed of individuals who will have different reasons for voting the way they do.

When the time to decide comes, they will each go into their mental closets, pull out the one or two issues that concern them the most, and vote for the vendor who addressed them to their satisfaction. "Not fair!" you say. "Not relevant," we respond. Whoever said life was fair? "Those deciding issues might not even be the most important ones to the company!" you say. True. Maybe that knowledge *should* change their votes, but it won't. When it comes time to vote, *personal* issues outweigh corporate ones.

It's easy to find out what the corporate issues are. It takes a bit more skill to uncover personal issues. Sheila was shot down by a competitive samurai because she didn't know the personal issues! Her competitor helped the prospect pick the issues—the very ones that favored him! That's the secret to competitive selling. **Control the issues and you control the sale.** Help the prospect select the pivotal issues, those that act like kindling to his emotions and can blaze into a fire only you can extinguish. Most of your competitors won't know what the real issues are, and they'll be dumping wheelbarrows of features and functions on the prospect, completely unaware that they are overlooking the key issues. They won't know what's happened until you've left with the contract in your pocket.

An old American proverb says, "Never look for the birds of this year in the nests of the last." You should never assume that yesterday's issues are today's issues.

When you get close to the decision date, strange

things begin to happen. Prospects start changing issues. They'll drop old ones and pick up new ones. As you get closer to decision time, the pace of change can become almost frantic. Real estate agents see this on a daily basis. It probably happened to you the last time you made a major purchase. As a samurai salesman, you'll want to stay close to the prospect during these final days. Don't leave anything to chance. Let them know through your demeanor that you are there, that you are confident, that you will help them, that you will serve.

Get them to talk about the future, when they will be using your product or service, and get them to tell you how life will be for them then! This shifts the focus from "pre-sale jitters" to "post-sale joy." In other words, they're already mentally using yours while your competitor is still doing "show and tell."

In picking the issues, remember that the only issue that matters is one that has great emotion for the prospect and one that shows your strengths! Consequently, you'll naturally give a lot of thought to the issues that play into your hand and favor your position. We're not talking about mere technical issues like product features. The issues you choose must carry emotional energy. Remember, it is not enough to win their *heads*, you must win their *hearts*.

Many salespeople make the mistake of relying solely on their product's perceived strengths to make the sale. This is not enough to win. You must see how your prospect is reacting to this strength. Worse, your competitor already knows your strength and may be attacking it. Read your prospect's reactions carefully before deciding which issues are important. Once you have discovered these issues, you'll be on the inside track. If you are skillful in disguising your battle plan, you'll find that your competition is wasting time fighting over issues that the prospect doesn't even think particularly important. This happened to Sheila. Don't let it happen to you.

The redoubtable General Sun Tsu wrote, "*The spot where we intend to fight must not be made known, for then the enemy will have to prepare against a possible attack at several different points.*" He was writing, of course, about actual conflict, but his advice is apropos for business conflicts as well.

There are times, of course, when you *must* fight from a well-known position. Even then, however, it is possible to fight a far different battle from what your adversary is expecting—as we learn in the story that follows!

A LESSON FROM THE ANCIENT SAMURAI

The enemy had surrounded the fortress, knowing that they vastly outnumbered the samurai who were in charge of its defense. First, they attacked the walls of the fortress, throwing grappling hooks to the top and climbing up, preparing to do battle. The samurai, however, had prepared a false wall that was supported by ropes, inside the compound. Once their enemies were at the top, they simply slashed the restraining ropes, and the wall fell on the attackers, killing more than a thousand of them.

The leader of the attacking force ordered another assault. "The moat is shallow, and the real wall is not as tall as the false wall we climbed before," he said. But his army was hesitant, wondering if that wall would fall on them, as well.

Obediently, yet fearfully, the attackers waded into the moat and again threw grappling hooks and began their climb. The defenders poured boiling water on their adversaries and again decimated them. The attackers regrouped and came again, only to find that the second wall was also a false wall and yet another wall lay before them.

The samurai in the fortress knew in advance that

their enemies would attack their strongest position. Yet, by defending their positions with imagination and determination, they were able to eventually win the day.[10]

3. Direct the Battle

Once you've chosen the battleground (i.e., the buying issues with enough emotional energy to drive a decision), you will want to step back and direct the battle as it unfolds. Think of yourself as a movie director and of the issues as the various scenes in your story. A good movie director knows just how he or she wants the audience to feel at the beginning and end of each scene. How do you want your prospect to feel as each issue unfolds in the theater of her mind? Well, you want her to feel like s*he wants to feel*!

Most prospects view their most important issues with one of two reactions: fear or joy. Ordinarily we want to soothe fears and build on joys, but there are exceptions that "prove" every rule. Suppose you're offering a hospital a new piece of diagnostic gear that is a quantum leap ahead of MRI or Catscan. Obviously the "newness" of your gear is an issue. Well, one prospect might feel fear about that newness. He perceives that the technology may be new and unproven, and should it fail to meet expectations, he will be embarrassed, ridiculed, or even discharged. Another prospect might look at the newness issue with joy, feeling that she will be perceived as a forward-thinker, a pioneer on the leading edge of technology.

10. From the Taikeika.

Tale of a Modern Samurai

Say your prospect feels fear over an issue. You must either remove that fear or remove that issue from the decision-making process. Marc was presenting a proposal for a safety seminar to a major, multinational corporation. His prospect was fearful that weaving a bit of humor into the two-day program would make the program appear frivolous. Knowing that his competitor did straightforward presentations that were technically correct but somewhat boring, Marc did not feel he should try and compete in that arena. Besides, he knew that while the students had to attend in body. If the presentation was boring, they'd all send their minds out for a sandwich.

Marc said, "I can see that you're concerned about using humor, and I want to resolve that issue. Since this is our first project together, I want you to be comfortable. But, more than that, I want you to be successful. I believe the humor acts as mental hooks to hold the concepts we want to share. Before you make your final decision, let me write you a straightforward presentation and add some short, humorous films we can weave in and out of the seminar to drive home our points. Then, we'll test it on your trainers. If they don't agree that the humor adds to the presentation, we can remove it, and we'll still have a program as good as anything currently in your inventory."

By offering the humor as an option and minimizing their fear (they could always take it out), Marc helped the client see that it did, indeed, add to the program. Humor became a key swing issue in their decision. The program was produced as written and became the highest-rated seminar of the year!

When you direct the battle scenes, you are calling the tune. Your competitor must now dance to your tune and when the competition starts to hum your tune, he has to play second fiddle. When Marc made humor an issue in his sales call, the competitor was at a fatal disadvantage, because the prospect's initial fear of humor had turned to joy.

A LESSON FROM THE ANCIENT SAMURAI

Musashi wrote, "You must move your opponent's attitude. Attack where his spirit is lax. Throw him into confusion; irritate and terrify him. Take advantage of the enemy's rhythm when he is unsettled, and you will win the battle."

This advice was taken to heart by the Samurai Nobunaga (1534–82) during the invasion of Korea. When the Korean army began fleeing, Nobunaga told his soldiers not to pursue them, but to follow at a long distance. "We will overtake them just before they get to a main city," he advised, "then we will have them and their provisions!" Nobunaga not only beat them, he used them to transport his provisions to the city where he needed them!

4. Prepare for Battle

In any kind of battle the best surprise is *no* surprise! The best way to avoid unpleasant surprises is to prepare for all the contingencies beforehand. The first step in this preparation is to arm yourself with knowledge. Knowledge begins with understanding yourself, your company, and your product or service.

Yet, no samurai can achieve maximum success unless he also knows his competitor! Because knowing your enemy is vitally important, we've attached a form at the end of this chapter that will aid you in understanding those you're competing against. The form will guide you through questions like "Where are they weak? Where are they vulnerable? Where are they strong?"

In addition to thinking about the rival company, you also need to think about the salesperson who will be competing with you for the sale. What issues will he or she bring up in fighting against you? Put those issues on the paper, too, and prepare to handle them.

You also need to think about your prospect. On a separate piece of paper, put down what your prospect needs and wants. Remember: when in doubt—*ask*. Remember, too, that in spite of your best Ben Duffy–type efforts,[11] the prospect's list of what he needs may be different from your list of what he needs. What do you do to resolve the conflict? Simple. Remember that his list is more important than yours—so use it instead of your own. When Chuck made a large sale for his company years ago, his manager asked, "Why did they buy from us?" When Chuck told him, the manager gasped, *"But they bought for the wrong reasons!"* Chuck simply smiled and said, "No, they bought for the *right* reasons—*theirs!"*

Once you've anticipated the actions and reactions of the competitive company, the competitive salesperson, and your prospect, you're ready to plan your attack. Often you'll attack where your competition is weak. However, unless this is a new weakness, they may have developed a pretty good method of disguising it.

Never discount the advantage of striking directly at their stronghold! Sometimes a competitor has one point that is so strong that no one has ever dared attack it. This could mean that they haven't a battle plan to defend it, and you can be victorious! On the surface, attacking a competitive stronghold sounds illogical and hopeless. Yet, it can flow like this:

Their strength, which uncovers ➡ Their weakness, which shows ➡ Your strength.

We can recall more than one example of where David

11. Ben Duffy's the advertising genius we told you about in Chapter 3, the one who made a list of the questions his prospect would probably want to ask *him*!

not only attacked Goliath and won, but attacked at Goliath's strongest point: his size! A small software company with *only three customers* won a major sale against one of the largest software companies in the world. The salesperson from the big company got a bit complacent because he couldn't conceive of a situation in which an account would select an upstart over an industry leader. He went into shock when the contract went to the little guy! How did David topple Goliath? He went into the account and said, "Oh, you don't want to use *that company*! Most of their customers are in Europe and you know those Europeans, they just do things differently than we do. Of the hundreds of clients they have here in the USA, very few are like you. We know how to service you better, because all our clients are just like you! Go with us. We're small enough to give you the personal service you want and need on this project. Let's work together!" It worked!

This is an excellent example of samurai-selling. Samurai David went right at the size of Goliath and won a million dollar deal. The prospect bought the "hometown expertise" and went with a local firm that only had three clients in the entire world!

The attack was so illogical, so farfetched, so *preposterous*, that the Goliath company was taken by surprise, and the battle was over before they knew why they had lost.

Admittedly, you shouldn't attack an enemy stronghold unless attacking that stronghold points out a weakness in their product or service and a corresponding strength in yours. For example, suppose you are selling a well-known product. Your strengths are that the product entails no risk and that your service is superb. You are facing a competitor who has a new product that is touted as "state of the art." (Though you know that it has yet to prove itself reliable.) They, of course, are painting a picture of your product as old, worn, and boring. If you make the obvious counterattack, talking up your strengths as being years in the business with a mature product, low risk, and a large client base, you play into their hands. Instead, consider making the issue how dangerous an "immature," unproven product can be (That's another way of saying "state of the art"!) and the dangers of a weak support network. Our product took years to develop and perfect, is wonderfully supported, and available today. After all, you are buying this to *solve problems*—not *create problems*! I wouldn't want to be the first one to have a heart operation using some new, yet-to-be-completely-developed heart valve technology if I didn't have to, would you?"

See how emotion came into play? By using metaphors and stories, you can attack through your prospect's feelings, leaving your competition out in the cold. Use your prospect's joys and fears to present your offering to better advantage.

A LESSON FROM THE ANCIENT SAMURAI

Musashi said, "Using the wisdom of strategy, think of the enemy as your own troops. When you think of him in this way, you can move him at will and be able to chase him around. You become the general, and the enemy becomes your troops." Another time, Musashi said, "The important thing in strategy is to suppress the enemy's useful actions while allowing his useless ones."

It is no wonder that the great Sun Tsu wrote, "A clever warrior not only wins, but wins with ease."

5. Watch for a Competitive Attack

The most effective attacks are surprise attacks—the

Japanese raid on Pearl Harbor, the Allied invasion at Normandy, or Schwarzkopf's brilliant end sweep around Kuwait. In Chapter 4, we told how General Li Ching's sneak attack surprised and routed his enemies. Napoleon said a forced march before a battle enhanced the chance of success, because the troops who were moving were prepared to fight, while those who were at ease were not. Selling is like chess in that you cannot concentrate on your own moves so totally that you become unaware of what the other side is doing. Just as you're preparing your victory celebration, your competitor may be leading a forced march to the prospect that will defeat you. What can you do? Well, you can't watch your competitor every day, but you can keep close watch on your prospect. Be wary of anything that might indicate a competitive inroad. There are two danger signals to watch for in the final days before a decision: (a) your prospect goes silent, or (b) your prospect starts firing new, semi-irrelevant objections.

If the prospect goes silent on you, you are in trouble, because it is a sure sign that your competitor has made some inroads and may well have planted some mine fields between you and the sale. Get in there, and find out what is happening. The best source of information is the silent prospect himself or someone close to him.

It doesn't matter whether you're selling insurance or investments, appliances or aluminum siding, posthole diggers or popcorn poppers. If your prospect starts giving you a bunch of weird objections, treat each objection as an opportunity to uncover the buying criteria. Above all, try to find out what the underlying emotional basis is behind those objections.

There's a lot of pressure on the prospect as the selling process moves to a close. That pressure is apt to come back to you. Take it all in stride, and no matter how frantic things become, remember the advice Lou gave Sheila: *A samurai never panics! Your calm, helpful, willing presence in the midst of the storm will show the prospect that you are the kind of person they want on their team after the sale.*

The human brain is funny. If it attaches emotion to an objection, it needs emotion to unseat it. The best way to handle this one is to create an analogy or a story that will help the prospect attach a new emotion to the issue.

An Example from a Modern Samurai

A salesman working for one of our clients was presenting his product to a prospect, and things were going well. Suddenly the atmosphere changed, and when probed, the prospect said, "I'm afraid to buy from your company because it's small, like three men in a garage."

The samurai was stunned, because nothing was farther from the truth. In fact, his was a multimillion dollar company with nearly a hundred employees. Yet, he was wise enough to know that you do not change someone's mind with facts if facts were not used in making up his mind. The samurai merely smiled. "John, you know we're not three men in a garage. Sure, this company was started by three men, but today we're a strong, healthy company. Still, it's no disgrace to be just three men in a garage. After all, from one man in a garage came the electric light bulb. From two men in a garage came the airplane. Just imagine what three men in a garage could do!"

By using his simple analogy, gentleness, and humor, the samurai calmed a minor objection and a major emotion. Later, when the competitor came back and repeated the "three men in a garage" story, the prospect smiled and said, "You know, *three* men in a garage created Apple Computer!" While the salesman mulled that over, the prospect announced that he had decided to buy from our little client!

CREATE AN ACCOUNT
CONTROL DOCUMENT

In selling today, even the best-planned battlefield can get very complicated, very quickly. Decision making is never simple, and the greater the number of people involved, the more complex it becomes. Your prospect (or prospect committee) is getting assurance from you and pressure from their peers, their superiors, and your competitors. In military battles, commanders use maps and charts to help them keep track of friendly and enemy movements. In business battles, we must do the same.

In Corporate Vision's Samurai Selling Seminar, we developed an easy-to-use Account Control Document. We have found it a great help in monitoring current and changing conditions on the sales battlefield. On this document you list all the people involved in the decision, what you know about them, and how you will sell them. You must list all the issues that are important to each of these people. Then you'll need to determine how you'll ensure that these issues favor you and how you can create the emotional energy in the prospect that will cause him to decide that your solution is the right one.

Remember, this is a tool, not a talisman. Don't become a slave to the document. Create your own, one that fits your needs. Keep it short, but make it work for you. If you have done everything else properly, these steps should enable you to go into any competitive situation and to win.

The Account Control Document is reproduced on the following three pages.

ACCOUNT CONTROL DOCUMENT

ACCOUNT: City/State _____

BASIC ACCCOUNT INFORMATION: Phone:

Major Competitors	Their Positioning	Your Strategy
_____	_____	_____
_____	_____	_____
_____	_____	_____

DECISION PROCESS Decision Date: _____   Install Date:_____

Event	Target Date	Your Goals and Objectives
_____	_____	_____
_____	_____	_____
_____	_____	_____
_____	_____	_____
_____	_____	_____
_____	_____	_____

KEY PLAYER/Title *Role* _____   *Personal Issues*

_____	Approves Deal	_____
_____	Decision Maker	_____
_____	Influences Decision	_____
_____	Influences Decision	_____
_____	Influences Decision	_____
_____	_____	_____
_____	_____	_____
_____	_____	_____

Reason they need your solution:

Sales obstacles that can stall the sale:

Basic strategy to close this account:

KEY PLAYER IN DECISION

Name _____ Title _____

Role in decision: (e.g., decision maker, approves contract, key user, technical evaluator, etc.)

What do you need to win this person's vote?

How will this person win with your solution?

How can you dramatize it for this person?

What benefit can this person get by *not* buying your product or service?

Will this person hinder the decision? How, why, and what can you do about it?

What pain/nuisance issues can you solve for this person?

How can you contrast the old way from your new way?

How can you make benefits vivid and specific to this person?

What battleground issues can you create for a competitive advantage?

When is the best time for you to introduce these issues?

Are there any obstacles and objections important to this person that you must handle now?

What this buyer thinks of the key competitors:

Competitor	Likes	Dislikes
Current Supplier		
Competitor #1		
Competitor #2		
Your solution		

Lou Capps, Modern Samurai (concluded)

When Lou had finished going over the competitive steps, Sheila set her coffee cup down on the table and nodded thoughtfully. "I can see now all the competitive steps I should have taken, Dad, but what am I going to do now? My competitor won, and it's a 'done-deal.'"

"Not necessarily," Lou said. "The good part is that the anguish of decision making is over now. That is better than dealing with a client who can't seem to make up his mind! Yet, in spite of what you and your prospect think, they may not have made their decision.

"You know, Sheila, you and I both like baseball—"

"We never missed the opening game!"

"Right. And we always hear people say, 'Three strikes and you're out!' Well, that's true in baseball, but it isn't true in selling. The truth is, you can come right back up to the plate after having struck out and ask for another pitch! Nobody can put you out of the game until you're ready to admit you're defeated."

"What are you suggesting?" she asked.

"Call and ask them if they'd do you a personal favor and share why they decided the way they did. Tell them this would be a gift to you, so you won't make the same error next time. If you're nonthreatening and sincere, and if they like you—and we know they do—they'll give you an audience.

"When you go in, keep the beginner's mind. Be innocent. Keep the meeting open and matter-of-fact. Ask simple questions, and don't interrogate them or be anxious. If they feel they're having to defend their decision, they'll clam up on you. Ask them why they made the decision they did. Listen politely, and as a friend who wants to serve, dig down just a bit below the surface. After you're comfortable that you know the facts, repeat them, and ask if you understand their reasons correctly. Once they agree, ask, "If this were not the case, then I would have won, wouldn't I?" The answer will invariably be yes.

"Then get them to tell you what they liked about your

program. Get them to concur with your strengths. Ask them if, except for those issues mentioned, they really wanted your product. If they answer yes, and they often do, get their permission to work on these issues and then go for it!"

Lou picked up his fork and cut into his cheesecake. *"You do that, and you have a good shot at winning!"*

"Do you really think so, Dad?"

Lou took a bite of blueberry cheesecake. *"It's a piece of cake, Sheila. After all, they've just told you, line by line, what you have to do to get the business. Now you don't even have a competitor to worry about, because like the rabbit in the story, he's asleep on the road thinking he's won—while you, you little stealth samurai–ninja turtle, sneak right past him to the finish line."*

"I dunno," Sheila said thoughtfully. *"It sounds easy, but what are the odds?"*

Lou laughed, *"Ten percent of my annual sales come from 'lost' deals!"*

Chapter 6: Self-Check Exercise

1. Pick a competitor on a current sale:

    A. What are their apparent strengths?

    B. What are their weaknesses?

    C. How can you attack their strengths in a way that highlights their weaknesses and your strengths?

2. Who is the salesperson for this competitor?

   A. How is this person likely to attack?

   B. How will you handle that attack?

3. What common objection do you find hard to handle?

4. Can you create a response that uses a story or analogy to turn this objection into a benefit?

   Objection   *Analogy*

5. If a prospect prefers an exciting competitive product to yours, one even a little risky, how will you position your offering?

POWER

DEMONSTRATIONS

ANYONE WHOSE KNOWLEDGE of samurai comes from the Japanese samurai movies or their westernized counter-parts[12] might get the idea that all a samurai did was fight. While a samurai's service often included combat, the ideal situation was to win the cause without blood-shed. A truly great samurai, as we reported earlier, could often win battles based simply on his *ki*, his inner

12. The Hollywood epic *The Magnificent Seven* was a western-ized version of the movie *The Seven Samurai*.

strength. If the inner person was right, then that confidence was mirrored in the way the samurai carried himself, the ease and familiarity with which he handled his weapons, his calm assurance as he approached the competition. His confidence served to put the competition on notice that this was no person to trifle with.

As a modern samurai, all the skills you have developed through the other chapters should give you deep confidence as you approach the key moment: demonstrating your product or service. Your demo is important, whether you're selling an automobile, a computer system, airplane, appliance, investment opportunity, insurance program, a mattress, baldness remedy, or what-have-you. This is where the rubber meets the road, the solution meets the problem.

All of the other conversations you may have with the buyer are limited, because the buyer must constantly try to imagine using your product. Now he gets to actually see it with his own eyes, touch it with his own hands, and experience it directly. You've heard the adage, "A picture is worth a thousand words," and it's true. Well, a demonstration is worth ten thousand words because recent research shows that our brains act a hundred times faster on what we see than they do on what we imagine.

We have interviewed hundreds of prospects for our clients and found that a high percentage of them chose to buy or not to buy during the product demonstration. Therefore, your demo must visually show your product solving problems, increasing productivity, providing happiness, minimizing fear, and improving lives. We do this by finding the problem areas our product can address and expanding them, making them come alive as we discussed in the section on Creating a Sense of Urgency. We not only discover the *problems,* but the *effects of the problems.*

You must make solving those problems important to the buyer, because often the buyer has lived with a problem so long that he's forgotten what it was like to be problem-free. Chances are, the problem grew in intensity over time, and he has gotten almost accustomed to the pressure. How is it possible to get accustomed to pressure? Well, in a classic lab experiment a live frog is in a pan of lukewarm water on a lighted stove. If the water is heated too quickly, the frog gets uncomfortable and simply jumps out. However, if the heat is applied gradually, the frog adjusts to the change and sits there in the pan as the water slowly gets hotter and hotter—until he is cooked! It is important to remember that, at any time, the frog could have escaped, but because the unpleasant change happened gradually, he never noticed how uncomfortable he was until it was too late. At the end, he literally stewed in his own ignorance.

If the prospect's problems had occurred quickly, he would have jumped at your solution. But since problems usually occur over time, he has gotten accustomed to being a bit uncomfortable. During the demo you'll want to restore the real level of nuisance and pain. You'll want to make the water hot, the consequences plain, and the promised relief believable and desirable. Then you'll want to contrast the effect of the problem to the effect that will come when the problem is solved!

An ordinary salesman is so interested in "the pitch" that he isn't aware that the buyer has gotten accustomed to living in a pan of water that's steadily getting warmer and warmer. A samurai salesman, who has a "fire raging through his hair," has a sense of urgency about solving the prospect's problem, and he infects the prospect with it. The samurai vividly warns, "It's uncomfortable! It's HOT! It's going to kill you if you don't DO SOME-THING!"

The ordinary salesperson tries to convince the prospect-frog with rhetoric and rationale, functions and features. The samurai paints pictures of how hot it is, of how much hotter it is going to get, and of what the ultimate outcome will be if something isn't done! The prospect begins to feel the heat, he begins to dread the outcome, if he doesn't act now.

Whatever your product or service, there are five secrets of a successful demo that every samurai should know:

1. Create strong, emotional moments to mark the prospect's mind.
2. Make the complex simple to understand.
3. Bewitch 'em; don't bore 'em.
4. Make it vivid, specific, personal, and concrete.
5. Get public positive feedback from your prospect.

Remember, a demo is a *selling* event, not a *telling* event, so you want to use all your persuasive powers!

Story of a Modern Samurai

When Chuck was a teenager, he sold furnace cleanings during a summer break. People don't worry much about their furnace during the summer, so he and a team of six other teenagers had their work cut out as they went from door to door explaining their service. The boys sold a lot of cleanings, but they also made a list of all the houses that had a coal furnace that didn't buy a cleaning.

At the end of the summer a samurai salesman from the company's headquarters drove up in a long Cadillac and called on every home with a coal furnace that had not purchased a cleaning. The man made a presentation on the kind of work his company did and the value of a clean furnace. Then he capped it off with a demo. He opened a jar of soot, poured a bit in his hand, lit a match and dropped the lit match in his hand. As the fire blazed on top of the soot, the salesman said calmly, "You'll notice that the soot is insulating my hand. That's what's happening in your furnace. Soot—like you have built up in your furnace—is a good insulator. That means that most of the heat from the coal you're burning is going up the flue and not getting into your home. Once we've cleaned your furnace, you'll be getting all the heat you're paying for!" He made almost every sale!

Now that you have the five secrets, let's look at each separately.

1. Create Emotional Moments to Mark the Prospect's Mind

Emotional moments mark the mind. Think back over the strongest memories of your own life. Don't they all have strong emotion attached? The mind considers emotion to be such a priority that it even uses different neural pathways to store emotions from those used for facts. Retention of emotion is part of our survival mechanism.

For instance, many people say they dislike history because "It's boring." Frankly, most history is boring because historians like to focus on names, dates, and statistics rather than stories and emotions. Yet, those same people who claimed to be bored with history sat and watch the PBS miniseries on the Civil War. This was not only one of the top-rated shows of the season; even though the program ran free on television, so many wanted to see it again that Time-Life successfully sold the tapes! Since most people don't like history, why did they love this particular historical program? Because the program used old photos, letters, and diaries to demonstrate the drama and emotion inherent in the conflict. We are drawn to and remember emotion; we tend to forget facts.

You can capture EMOTION with:	You'll LOSE SALES with:
Vivid	Statistical
Specific	General
Personal	Impersonal
Concrete	Abstract

If you say to most salespeople, "Sell to the emotion," they'll quickly assure you that they do just that! But if you could be a mouse in the corner during one of their calls, you would see and hear something very different. Most salespeople think that "Sell to the emotion" means to "give the prospect a warm, fuzzy feeling toward you and your company."

Ordinary salespeople think, "If I just keep monitoring their general attitude toward our product and make sure everyone is pleased, I'm selling to their emotions." If you're thinking that's all there is to selling to their emotions, then you're dead wrong. What do you think the competition is doing—trying to tick them off?

When you play this type of ordinary sales game, you are playing right into the hands of the competitor! Let's change the game. Let's sell the samurai way.

Create emotional moments, things that explode like land mines when they are stepped on. For example, if the prospect has a recurring nuisance problem that he has to address periodically, tie your solutions to that event. When the problem resurfaces, as it will, he'll be annoyed and mentally flash back to your solution and think to himself, "I've really got to get that solution!"

When Marc was having trouble with his dishwasher, he complained to the service person, "It always seems to go out on holidays when no one wants to work on it." The service man said, "Buy one from me, and I'll provide same-day warranty maintenance for a full year." Mark didn't buy then, but the next time the dishwasher went out (on Thanksgiving Day, naturally!), he remembered the man who had offered a solution to his problem, and he bought!

Ask yourself, "What really excites *me* about my product and company?" Write down the three most important reasons YOU would buy this product instead of a competitor's.

1.

2.

3.

Now ask yourself, "How can I *dramatically* generate that same kind of excitement in my prospect?" Think like a movie director, not a history professor. Now look at your reasons and jot down ways to dramatize them.

	How to
Reason:	*Dramatize It:*
1.	
2.	
3.	

At the end of each call, ask yourself, "Did I create some powerful 'emotional markers' during this call? Have I made sure that key features/issues will stick with the buyer? What other markers do I need to create?"

2. Make the Complex Simple

A famous sales motivator once observed, "Samson killed a thousand men with the jawbone of an ass. Ten times that many sales are killed each day with the same instrument!" While admitting the remark was filled with humor and hyperbole, the speaker used it to make a valid point. Yet, the jawbone that kills sales is wielded with the best of intentions. Most salespeople talk until everyone is totally confused, and then they ask for the order!

We might enjoy chaos on stage or at a soccer match, but when we are learning about something or trying to make an important decision, the mind desperately seeks *order* and *simplicity*. Confusion kills sales.

You may well ask, "How do I achieve order and simplicity if I'm selling a very complex product? If I don't tell *everything*, won't I be in danger of losing the sale? Don't they need to be fully informed to make a decision?"

The more complex your product, the more you need to *simplify the issues*. If it's complex and comprehensive, you can easily be pulled into sounding like a walking encyclopedia unless you have a different goal. You'll overload people with information and see your sales cycle lengthen. Prospects will say things like:

> "Well, we've decided this is a bigger decision than we thought. We'll need to form a committee and set up guidelines, etc."

> "It looks good, but we need to research the market more. We'll get back to you."

Many salespeople hear remarks like these every day, never suspecting that what the prospect is really saying is, "Now I'm confused and scared of making a mistake. This is more complicated than I thought. I'm going to need more time to sort this out!" He's beginning to feel as Mark Twain did when he wrote, "[They] have already thrown much darkness on this subject, and it is probable that, if they continue, we shall soon know nothing at all about it."

The samurai salesman is a master of making complicated things sound simple and dull things sound exciting. Here is a samurai secret to help you mentally manage the buying process: Start with **The Big Picture**.

The mind automatically tries to categorize all incoming information. It asks, "Where shall I put this information? Is this about dogs, trucks, alligators, computers, etc.?"

Read the following paragraph. Notice how you struggle to understand Robert Ornstein's classic prose below:[13]

> With hocked gems financing him, our hero bravely defied all scornful laughter that tried to prevent his scheme. "Your eyes deceive," he had said. "An egg, not a table, correctly typifies this unexplored planet." Now three sturdy sisters sought proof. Forging along, sometimes through calm vastness, yet more often very turbulent peaks and valleys, days became weeks as many doubters spread fearful rumors about the edge. At last from nowhere welcome winged creatures appeared, signifying momentous success.

There are two problems with the preceding. First, the language is a bit stilted. Secondly, we were never given the Big Picture. Here's the Big Picture: We are talking about Columbus's voyage of discovery. Now go back and read the preceding paragraph again and see how much clearer it becomes!

All the little details come into sharper focus once we've seen the Big Picture. We have to give the mind a place to store the information and an easy way to evaluate it. In movie-making, they call it the "establishing shot." For instance, in the motion picture *The Sound of Music*, we open with an establishing shot of the Alps with snowy peaks and green meadows covered with wild flowers. We immediately know where we are—and are prepared to learn that "the hills are alive with the sound of music!" Your prospect deserves an establishing shot, a glimpse of the Big Picture before you get

13. Robert Ornstein, *The Evolution of Consciousness* (Englewood Cliffs, N.J., Prentice-Hall, 1991), p. 187.

into details. A confused prospect will not buy. The only emotions a confused prospect feels are fear, helplessness, and irritation—not the buying emotions.

Ordinary salespeople are often afraid to make it simple. They think the prospects will consider it condescending! If it smacks of arrogance, they will. Otherwise, they'll respect you for it. After all, no one was ever hired to make things more complex, but we frequently hire people to make complex things more simple. People appreciate a quick, simple overview before you begin.

In a recent seminar a salesman took a complex issue and made it simple and fun to learn about by drawing on an overhead transparency. He sketched a small island with a man leaning against a palm tree. He told us that many companies have been leaning back in the sun, thinking that they own the market. He then added just two things that totally changed the picture: a dark cloud, and sharks circling in the water!

When you determine to make it simple, you have to edit. When you edit, you remove everything but the core issues and then ask yourself, "How can I make this interesting, dramatic, and easy to remember?" That keeps you from pouring in tons of useless information that only bogs down the sale.

An Example from a Modern Samurai

One of our clients had an information system for hospitals but found that no one attached any importance to what they considered their proudest feature: a relational database. That capability tied all the activities that occur in the hospital into one coherent information system. They later discovered that, no matter how long they explained it, prospects had difficulty grasping exactly what a "relational database" was and why it was important. They solved the problem with a simple graphic, a pyramid.

First, they showed the prospect a pyramid and said, "Okay, this is your hospital and all its separate departments.

It doesn't matter whether you're a doctor, a nurse, an admin-
istrator, or the head of admissions, you feel like you are at the
top of the pyramid and everyone else is below you." Their
next visual showed the same pyramid with a ball in the mid-
dle. The speaker now said, "This ball represents the central
information core of the system. When you put any patient
information into the computer, it is stored in this central
core. When anyone else puts any patient information into the
computer, it also goes to this core. Since this core is cen-
tral, all the information can be shared by all authorized users.
For instance, if you're the doctor and you need the patient's
home address or medical record, you can get it. If you're in
accounting and you need to know what procedures were
administered, you can get those, too. Everyone shares the
same information, so you never get told, "You'll have to go
over to such-and-such department for that information!" We
call that central information core a "relational database."
You'll call it wonderful, because you'll have all the informa-
tion you need at your fingertips with no hassle.

You could almost hear the audience gasp, "Ohhhh!
Wow!" Of course, this oversimplified a complex concept, but
its simplicity allowed the prospects to comprehend its incredi-
ble value. Naturally, they bought the system. (We know
samurai salesmen hate sales stories that don't have happy
endings!)

3. Bewitch 'Em; Don't Bore 'Em

After you've presented a clear, simple big picture, your
next samurai move is to make it as exciting as possible as
soon as possible. Save the mundane, everybody's-prod-
uct-has-one-of-these features for later... much later.

The brain is wide awake and alert at the *beginning* of
anything, slows down in the middle, and then perks up
toward the end (usually when it hears an audience's
two favorite words, "In conclusion"). When researchers
gave students a list of words to read only once, the
students remembered 70 percent of the words at the
beginning of the list, 20 percent in the middle, and 100

percent at the end. The fact that they remembered the words at the end isn't surprising, because they were the last they had read. What was surprising was that they only remembered one word in five out of the middle, yet remembered 70 percent of the *first* words! Logically, you would think that the first words would be the least remembered. Yet, our brains are so alert for beginnings that the first words were retained through a tedious and mostly forgotten middle.

How about you? Don't you remember your first date? Your first kiss? Your first car? How about your *third* date, kiss, or car?

Since everyone's brain is geared to remember firsts, let's show it something snazzy, something worth waking up for, something that says "Wow! This is different and exciting. I wish I had one *now!*"

When you normally demonstrate your product, what do people get most excited about? Whatever it is: **Do it first!** Don't let it get lost in that middle no-man's-land.

Not only do we want the first peeks at our product to be *exciting*, we also want the prospect to *feel the joy* of having it and using it. Don't aim for educating them, aim for the *thrill* of ownership! To help the prospect get that feeling, avoid static, passive phrases like "This feature allows you to ...," or "This product has these features...," or "The output parameters of the input paradyne are directly related...." Statements like these would not only put a cup of caffeine to sleep, they would shut down the most active brain in the universe!

Use active, dynamic phrases that involve the prospect and help her experience the product. Use phrases like "You will be able to . . ." and "Just imagine that your boss walks in tomorrow and asks for that 'Report from Hell' that always takes you two days to do—and she wants it yesterday. Let's see how you'll do it with our product!"

This is the prospect's opportunity to test-drive your product. Make it as much fun as driving a Maserati!

Sometimes salespeople of the non-samurai variety like to lead off with the boring in hopes that their presentation will "build to a climax" at the end. The problem is, if you begin your demonstration with a long, boring dissertation on your company's history, followed by a bucketload of facts, your prospect may be sound asleep before you get to the exciting stuff.

Earlier, we talked about the fact that people tend to remember only beginnings and endings. There is research, however, that would indicate that people tend to ignore *all data* when they are given more than they can process. Recently, neuroscientists tested people for the effects of information overload and found these common symptoms:

1. Irritation
2. Boredom
3. Inability to take decisive action
4. Pervading sense of "So What?"
5. Failure to respond

Can you think of a worse state of mind for your prospect to have at the end of your presentation?

4. Make it Vivid, Specific,
Personal, and Concrete

Our brains are neurologically wired to respond much more powerfully to vivid, specific, personal, and concrete information than to abstract data. Here's a statistic: 501 people were killed in Dallas in 1991. That's a terrible statistic, but it's just a fact, isn't it? After you read it, you might think about it for a few seconds, but then you're ready to go on to something else.

Now let's take that statistic and make it vivid, specific, personal, and concrete. Think of a place you know that would hold 501 people, maybe your church, a school auditorium, or a large theater. Imagine 501 people are in that building—kids, babies, grandmothers, brothers, and sisters, etc. Now imagine a deranged terrorist suddenly enters the room dressed completely in black, wearing a ski mask. He grabs your arm. You are going to have to stand beside him, point to each person, hand him each bullet, and watch at close range as he shoots all 501 people with his rifle—one at a time.

Notice how differently you feel about that number 501. You may feel sadness, fear, anger, a variety of emotions, but suddenly that statistic has become much more alive and dynamic for you. You feel much more involved than you were before. The statistic is the same: 501 deaths. The only change is that we made it **vivid, specific, personal,** *and* **concrete**.

Marc's pastor tells the story of a minister who stood before his congregation and said, "I have but three points to make today: (1) Thirty percent of the people in this city are going to Hell. (2) Eighty percent of you don't give a damn. (3) Ninety-five percent of you are more upset about my saying 'damn' than you are about the fact that 30 percent of your friends are going to Hell!"

Let's look at how making it personal applies to you in sales. You can either present a group of lifeless, abstract statistics and features—or you can look for ways to present that same information in a vivid, specific, personal, and concrete manner.

An Example from a Modern Samurai

One of our software clients wanted to make the point that their system was easier to reprogram in today's rapidly changing banking industry than a competitive program. For their power demonstration, they went around the bank's conference room spreading out a thirty-page-long computer printout. The speaker then said, "That is the amount of code you have to write in our competitor's system to create a new bank service." He then picked up one sheet of paper and held it up. "And this is how much code you have to write to do the same thing with our system."

Think anyone had any trouble remembering the advantage of their system? He could have talked for an hour and communicated less. He was brief, and he was vivid, specific, personal, and concrete!

What techniques help you make one of your features vivid, specific, personal, and concrete?

A. STORIES

Use a real story from a current customer to dramatize a feature.

Example: Thelma Goes Home.

One client wanted to show how his product would save the prospect time and money. In his samurai research, he found that all competitors' systems were more cumbersome. To write a particular report, you had to sit there and monitor it. That meant that Thelma, who was in charge of this process, had to sit and nursemaid the equipment. Our samurai summed up the benefits of his product in six words: "With our system, Thelma goes home!" He paused and added, "In fact, this is so important that we have renamed the Reportwriter feature 'Thelma goes home!'" Everyone understood the benefit, especially Thelma, who voted to accept their package and then, uncharacteristically, went home.

B. VIDEO

Consider creating a short video of people who use the product, telling what it means to them. Be sure they give specific, colorful information, not just general statements like "We really like ABC. It works great for us." To establish credibility, use real people to endorse your product, and give real-world stories and examples showing how the product benefits the users. You can make a tremendous impact on prospects!

* * *

C. ANALOGIES AND METAPHORS

The mind is associative, constantly comparing the new with the old. Learn to help the prospect create the mental associations you want. Ask yourself, "What can I compare this to in the real world?" Have a repertoire of analogies and metaphors to help set the value of key issues.

Example: Competing Against a Competitor That Discounts.

Company A sells a product that is great, but the prospect considers it a bit expensive. By contrast, Company B sells a product that can do 80 percent of what Company A's product can do, and it's *half the price!* Company B was really eating into Company A's sales! Then we created a new analogy for Company A. The results were amazing! Here's the analogy: "Mr. Prospect, you know this is an important decision for you. This decision affects the very heart of your company, doesn't it? It is like having a heart operation! Now, do you want a 100 percent effective heart operation or an operation that's only 80 percent effective but costs less?" (Not surprisingly, when it was explained that way, practically no one wanted the discount operation!)

What are the key emotional issues of your sale? How can you relate them to something in everyday life so that the prospect can consider your point of view?

Analogies aimed at the prospect's emotions, like the one above, can turn the whole sale just as a rudder turns an ocean liner.

Samurai salespeople know that selling is the art of managing perceptions, and our minds are easily swayed by simple analogies and metaphors from life. They provide an indirect approach to gently persuading the mind to reconsider its position.

* * *

D. DRAW VIVID CONTRASTS

Don't assume that your prospects are drawing the real contrasts between their current way of doing things and the benefits of your new way. Help them see the difference between the old way and the new way.

Remind them of how complicated, cumbersome, burdensome, and bad the old way is.

● → ● → ● → ● → ● → ● → ● → ● → ●→ ● → ● → ● → ● → ● →
● → ● → ● → ● → ● → ● = Result

Now, contrast it against the new way of life with *your* products or service, as our client did in his presentation to the bank when he compared thirty pages of copy to a single page.

● → ● → ● → ● → ● → ● = Result

We need to see it to believe it! One salesman brought his son's toy building blocks from home and very creatively and simply showed a prospect the difference between the old way and the new way!

5. Get Public Positive Feedback

Robert Ornstein, in his book *The Evolution of Consciousness,* relates a story about a lunch he had with the mayor of San Francisco and a minister who headed a mission to help the less fortunate. They asked how the minister was able to recruit so many able helpers and to raise so much money. The minister explained that he had trained his workers to approach prosperous-looking people on the street during lunch and ask them to donate to the mission. Most refused. Then the worker would ask, "Would you just help us for five minutes folding and mailing a few letters for us at work?" Then the worker would offer five addressed, stamped envelopes and the letters, as well as a note about future work opportunities.

The minister said, "Just about everyone took the letters. And when they came back, they donated money, too! You know, once you get people involved, they'll stay involved!"

Studies show that once we make public statements, we are unlikely to change our minds. When you get a prospect to publicly endorse you, he or she is unlikely to withdraw that endorsement. By the same token, if you publicly commit yourself to a goal, whether it is family, personal, or professional, you aren't as likely to go back on it. (Remember our earlier story of our samurai salesman who, upon receiving his quota, immediately announced that his goal was to triple it!)

One reason we don't back down from a public statement is that it makes us look weak. This is a powerful weapon to use in your presentation. Don't let people simply sit passively through your sales presentation. Ask for public, positive feedback. Be sincere, let them tell you in their own words how they believe your product will help them. Those who give you that public feedback won't back down later, because they sense it would harm their credibility and their own sense of self-worth.

Research shows that once we publicly act or speak in favor of a subject, we tend to continue to support that position—without further evaluation. It is very difficult to retreat from a position you've voiced publicly.

How can we use this characteristic of basic human nature to help us sell more efficiently? In any sales call, and particularly during a demo of the product, watch for signs of positive reactions. When you see them nodding in agreement, asking questions enthusiastically, looking positively at each other, etc., *stop!* This is the perfect time to get **Public Positive Feedback**. Ask innocent, open-ended questions[14] such as:

14. An open-ended question is one that can't be answered with a simple yes or no, but requires an essay answer.

"Okay how do you do that here now?"

"Would it have any impact here at your company to be able to do this (feature)?"

"Tell me what, specifically, would be different here? How would this help you?"

Don't force an endorsement, let them share their insights with you. Let your prospect lead the way. Be genuinely curious about how your product will make a real difference to these people. Be nice, let them sell you! They will get excited, you will get excited, and that excitement will feed your *ki,* which, in turn, will feed everyone's excitement even more!

Ordinary salespeople notice these positive signals from prospects and just keep on pitching. They don't stop and use this powerful tool to lock in the buyer at the emotional moment when the buyer is saying positive things to himself. Learn to look for public positive feedback opportunities. Use them to win.

Remember: a demo is a *selling* event, not a *telling* event.

When all is said and done, it pays to remember that you have not arranged this demonstration just to educate and inform, but to encourage the prospect to take immediate action. In preplanning any demo, there are thousands of features and facts, benefits and bonanzas that you *could* tell them about. You must ruthlessly cast aside everything that encumbers you and take only what they need to know into the meeting. You won't go far afield if you remember that a demo is a *selling* event, not a *telling* event. This is no time to relive your kindergarten days when you come to school prepared for "show and *tell.*" These are your business days when you need to come ready to "show and *sell!*"

* * *

From the Files of Corporate Visions

A company phoned Corporate Visions to say they had just lost a $1.4 million corporate sale to a competitor, and they wanted to find out why. "Our company spent months on that account, and when a requisition for purchase was issued, we outscored every competitor by a wide margin! Yet, after the demo, they went with our competitor!"

Since Corporate Visions not only teaches sales techniques but conducts postmortems, they took the assignment. When they reached the decision maker, she told Karen, "We couldn't really see that much difference between the two companies, but the other company just made us feel more comfortable. I know it sounds silly, but we just liked *them better!"*

Following that revelation, the losing company signed up for Corporate Vision's Power Demos Workshop. Three months later, they were winning deal after deal against the same competitor. In fact, the turnaround was so dramatic that the competitor signed up for the course!

Moral: Give Power Demonstrations and those who see the difference you made will be your biggest boosters!

Chapter 7: Self-Check Quiz

In the space below, make a note of how you'll use the five secrets of a successful samurai demo to create a better demonstration of your product or service:

1. Pick a major feature of your product or service and create strong, emotional moments that mark the mind. Dramatize it, don't just talk it!

2. Take a complex concept about your product or service and simplify it.

3. How can you vividly contrast the new with the old?

4. Take a major benefit of your product or service and apply it to a top prospect, remembering to make it vivid, specific, personal, and concrete.

5. Create questions that will get you public positive feedback from your prospect.

    A.

    B.

    C.

6. List some ways you can add VSPC to your demon-stration:

    A. I'll make my demo *Vivid* by:

    B. I'll make my demo *Specific* by:

    C. I'll make my demo *Personal* by:

    D. I'll make my demo *Concrete* by:

7. Here are some ways I can keep my "show and *sell*" presentation from degenerating into a boring "show and *tell*" presentation:

    A.

    B.

    C.

    D.

THE SOUL

OF THE

SAMURAI

BY NOW YOU KNOW the skills you must possess to be a true samurai salesman. What remains is for you to go back and reread these lessons until they are locked into your heart, mind, and soul. The ancient samurai warrior wrote haiku, verse that gives the essence of feeling with a minimum of brush strokes. In the same tradition we have sought to be samurai writers, giving you the essence of what you must know to be a successful samurai salesman in as few words as possible.

Becoming a samurai, however, is not a one-time thing, but an *all-time* thing. You must continually purge yourself of everything that is not worthy of a samurai until you have acquired the soul of the samurai—that is, the soul of one who serves. In other words, service will become second nature to you, as natural as breathing.

Some 130-odd pages ago, we began a journey together. Our goal was to teach you the secrets of the samurai salesman; yours was to become the samurai you were meant to be.

We began by working on our *ki*, and said that our inner being must revolve around *a burning desire to serve*. When we have that kind of desire, we can defeat our adversaries even if they are better armed. *Ki*, you will recall, can stop a tank with nothing but a shopping bag.

A LESSON FROM THE SAMURAI

Musashi wrote down nine points that formed what he called "the way" to a perfect *ki*.

1. Do not think dishonestly.
2. The way is in training. Training is a part of your normal life.
3. Become acquainted with the arts. That is, don't become too tightly focused on one thing.
4. Know the ways of all professions.
5. Know the difference between gain and loss.
6. Develop intuitive judgment and understanding.
7. Perceive things that cannot be seen.
8. Pay attention to details.
9. Do not engage in useless activity.

Next we looked at the power of balance. A samurai salesman, like a samurai warrior, lives a life balanced by four virtues: integrity, discipline, creativity, and fear-lessness.

Integrity is many things. It is behaving with honor, never promising more than you can deliver, and keeping your commitments.

Discipline means realizing that every spectacular accomplishment is preceded by unspectacular preparation. It means learning all about your product and service and how each feature becomes a benefit for the prospect. It means refining your presentation skills and practicing so much that nothing "out of left field" can take you by surprise. It means living so in tune with your prospect that superlative performance becomes routine.

Creativity must always come after discipline. The most creative musician, writer, or samurai can only express creativity after mastering the basics. Only then is the mind of the samurai free to soar to new heights and to explore new horizons, new techniques, and new solutions.

We develop **fearlessness** by cultivating the *appearance* of fearlessness while working to master fear. The root of fear is often ignorance, and when we eliminate that, we open the door for fear to flee from our lives. How do you open the door for fear to flee? Simple. Cultivate integrity. Cultivate discipline. Cultivate creativity. When you have these three pillars of success firmly in place, there will be no place for fear in your life.

In Chapter 4, we learned the importance of keeping **a beginner's mind**. We must never get so jaded that we fail to see a world of fresh possibilities in every development. The way of the true master is to remain a student. You must master the techniques you will employ in selling, but don't become a slave to them. Innovate. Move outside the box. Explore new horizons.

To keep a beginner's mind, remember:

1. Keep an empty cup.
2. Always continue learning.
3. Be creative.
4. Don't get locked into technique.
5. Be here now.

It also helps if you can put yourself in the prospect's seat. That's the only perspective that counts.

In Chapter 5, we learned the importance of creating **a sense of urgency**. If you live "as though a fire were raging through your hair," you won't want to let the selling process dawdle. If you can "set your prospect's hair on fire," he or she won't, either! What does a person want when his hair is on fire—*an instant solution to the problem!*[15]

Time can quench the hottest prospect. When the fire dies down, the chance for victory dwindles. As Napoleon said, "A swift march enhances the morale of the army and increases its power for victory."

Urgency, of course, must be *genuine* urgency. False urgency, based on "limited time offers," "upcoming price increases," etc., are artificial. They will help get a prospect to buy now, but only if that prospect feels a genuine sense of urgency to buy your product or service in the first place.

One way to get a sense of urgency is to go APE. APE, you'll recall, is an acronym for:

Account questions.
Problem questions.
Effect questions.

You go APE by asking **account questions** to uncover the structure of the account. **Problem questions**

---

15. Please rest assured that we are speaking of figuratively setting your prospect's hair on fire.

uncover account problems. Then you dwell on the effects of those problems through the use of **effect questions**. The more your prospects meditate on the effects of their problems, the greater their sense of urgency! Soon they will be hot for a solution, and when you can smell their hair smoldering, you ask for the order!

In Chapter 6, we discussed the competitive samurai and the super-samurai's selling secrets. Remember them?

1. Know your competitor.
2. Pick the issues.
3. Prepare for battle.
4. Direct the battle.
5. Watch for a competitive attack.

In Chapter 7, we looked at power demonstrations. When you demonstrate your product or service, you're bringing to bear everything you've learned as a samurai. Everything else is now prologue, for your demonstration is where the rubber meets the road and the final buying decisions are made.

We've seen many sales killed with sensory overload. Avoid long, boring recitations of features without a single pinpoint of light played on how they would solve a client need. The result of sensory overload is confusion, not conversion. We quoted humorist Mark Twain's classic line earlier, but it bears repeating: "The researches of many commentators have already thrown much *darkness* on this subject, and it is probable that, if they continue, we shall soon know nothing at all about it." Which of us hasn't come out of a presentation knowing less than we knew going in? Have you ever suffered through a meeting that not only failed to provide light on areas where you were ignorant, but actually cast darkness onto things you thought you understood? We have! As presentations progress, all too often the prospect moves from enlightenment to total confusion as we bury them under a ton of facts. If your prospect must sit through a presentation like that, make certain it's your *competitor's presentation* and not yours! If you want the story to have a happy conclusion, you must remember to:

1. Create strong, emotional moments that mark the prospect's mind.
2. Make it simple, not complex.
3. Bewitch 'em; don't bore 'em.
4. Make it vivid, specific, personal, and concrete.
5. Get public positive feedback from your prospect.

NOW LET US LOOK AT THE SOUL OF THE SAMURAI

By the 1870s, Japan was united, the shoguns were gone, and modern firearms had made the sword of the samurai obsolete. Yet, everyone recognized the need for the continuation of the soul of the samurai—the soul of service. When Morihei Ueshiba founded aikido, the "loving martial art," samurai thinking went into the underlying philosophy.

Morihei said there were four spirits—water, earth, air, and fire—and that we could learn much from each.

- From **water**, the samurai learned fidelity, harmony, and propriety.
- From **earth**, the samurai learned love, compassion, and cherishing.
- From **air**, the samurai learned wisdom, light, and principle.
- From **fire**, the samurai learned valor, progress, and completion.

As samurai salesmen at the end of the twentieth

century, we too can learn from this philosophy. Let's explore the four "spirits" separately.

WHAT A SAMURAI
LEARNS FROM WATER

From water, we samurai learn that "everything changes." Water always reacts to its environment. It doesn't insist on its own shape but instead takes the shape of its container. Water can even change state, becoming ice, fog, steam, mist, dew. It can be a calm lake, a clear brook, a raging river, a flash flood, or a cool, refreshing drink on a hot, summer day. Yet it is still water, changing but changeless. Water is deceptively innocent in appearance, but it has the power to violently destroy homes or peacefully wear away the hardest stone!

Water has an unending list of qualities. It's the element that's essential for our physical health and well-being. Water covers more than 70 percent of our planet and forms 90 percent of our body weight. There is much a samurai can learn by studying water!

Fidelity

From water, a samurai learns to carry truth and fidelity as part of his being, letting them flow unfettered from a mind as clear and fresh as a mountain spring. Deceit muddies a clear mind just as horses muddy clear water. Kaishu, a master swordsman, recognized this and advised samurai to "keep the mind clear and serene like a bright mirror, and regardless of what occurs one will be able to deal with it in a natural, suitable manner."

Fidelity is a powerful attribute to bring to the sale. We've all met salespeople who were willing to tell you whatever you wanted to hear in order to get your money and to get on their way. Remember how you felt when you met that kind of salesperson? His lack of fidelity destroyed his relationship with you, didn't it? Even if a person like that makes a sale, he has not made an ally that will keep on doing business with him and refer him to friends!

Fidelity doesn't mean that you must tell the prospect about every little thing you think is a possible deficiency in your product or service. Quite often your opinion of these areas is very different from the prospect's. You don't tell your casual acquaintances about every wart, pimple, and flaw you have in order to show how truthful you are. The same is true in selling.

Mold your approach to fit the prospect; yet maintain your integrity. Water does that, doesn't it? It takes the shape of its holder, and yet it is still water!

Water is also known for its flexibility. Water bends and fills every crook and cranny it can. We should also learn to be flexible, easy to work with, pliable, and always seeking to take the shape of the problems and issues of our prospects. Flexibility is a major ingredient of sales success. Salespeople lose sales because their egos won't allow them to deviate from old positions and practices and look at the problem fresh. The samurai masters warned, "Resist becoming attached to one idea, one way of doing, one system. To do so is contrary to the laws of life."

We've watched sales people take sales training and then get locked into selling by a particular formula. This kind of thinking is dangerous. You must be flexible enough to fit into the prospect's mold, clear enough to mirror his hopes as a quiet pool mirrors the moon!

Harmony

With its fluid response, water seeks harmony in every situation, becoming one with those it serves. The ancient samurai said, "One has to become the situation, not separate oneself from it."

What causes us to lose our responsiveness and become rigid and combative when we're selling? Often it is because we have locked our minds onto a single path and lost our desire to create harmony for ourselves and our prospects. When a prospect feels we are pushing or pulling, he knows we aren't really listening and working diligently for his best interests.

A buyer recently told us, "I want a salesman to be someone I can trust—someone who I feel comfortable with, who tells the truth, even when the truth hurts or is ugly. I want him or her to be like a friend!"

From water we also learn not to keep account of slights or wrongs. Morihei Ueshiba was given this verse by his master as he completed the lessons:

All people know this!
When you strike
a flowing river,
no trace remains
in the water.[16]

The water doesn't strike back. It seeks harmony.

Propriety

From water, the samurai also learned propriety. *Webster's New Collegiate Dictionary* defines *propriety* as "the customs and manners of polite society." Samurai lived according to such strict guidelines that their code of politeness impelled some to commit *seppuku* (suicide) after offending another person. We aren't advocating that harsh a response today, but when the self-imposed penalty for impoliteness was so severe, few stepped over the boundaries.

16. Stevens, *Abundant Peace*, p. 12.

Minamoto Yoshite, an outstanding samurai of the twelfth century, politely placed each warrior in battle according to his performance the day before. This instilled such a sense of propriety among the samurai that it became a great honor to be in the greatest danger. During one battle an arrow struck a young samurai in the eye. A friend said, "Lie down, and I'll put my foot on your head and pull the arrow out!" "Certainly not!" the young samurai replied. "It is a greater indignity for a samurai to have a foot on his face than to lose an eye!"

This kind of adherence to customs and propriety may seem odd to us today, but there are some customs that are timeless. If you add to your selling skills the ability to find ways to express courtesy, compassion, and a generous spirit, those customs will never go out of style.

We know of one salesman (an ordinary one, not a samurai) who failed to learn this lesson. He arrived at the prospect's office with an assistant to give a product demonstration. While the demo was going on, the salesman excused himself, slipped out, and borrowed the secretary's phone to make calls to other prospects. He asked her for some coffee and even had her make copies for him. He didn't show the prospect the courtesy of finding out what his problems were or of even acting particularly interested in his own demonstration. That would be strange enough, but even stranger is the fact that the salesman was actually surprised when the prospect bought from someone else!

Generosity is another facet of propriety. In the sixteenth century, Tacite Shingen and Uesugi Kenshin were both noted for their generosity. Once, when Shingen's army ran out of salt, Kenshin heard of it and sent him some from his own supplies, even though they were adversaries. Shingen was so generous that he lived in an ordinary house instead of the traditional fortified castle. When asked about it, he said, "My castle is in the hearts of my people."

If you build your castle in the hearts of your prospects, no competitor can defeat you!

Yamaoku Tesshu (1836–88) was one of the last great samurai, bridging the gap from the age of the feuding shoguns to the formation of a single nation under the Meiji regime. Earlier, you read his extraordinary story of saving thousands of samurai lives by bravely entering the enemy camp and negotiating a surrender. Tesshu considered himself a "restorer" and founded a school called *Muto Ryu,* or "No-Sword." We encourage you to read the inspirational story of his life and philosophy in *The Sword of No-Sword* by John Stevens. His generosity, thoughtfulness, and sense of propriety was exceptional, and he did much to restore peace and harmony to his nation.

After the Meiji regime took the reins of government, Tesshu became the emperor's most trusted confidant and teacher. He received a handsome salary from the emperor, but he was always broke because he never turned anyone needy away from his door. Eventually he built a homeless shelter on his estate, and if the emperor gave him money for a new suit of clothes, he gave it to the needy.

Tesshu was truly "one who serves," not only in battle, but as a humanitarian in peacetime. In addition, he was also one of the greatest calligraphers in Japan's history. It is conservatively estimated that he produced a million works of art during the last eight years of his life. He didn't do it to become wealthy or famous; he did it to raise money to restore temples, help disaster victims, the hungry, and the homeless. There was such demand for his work that at one point his disciples had to hand out numbers to the dozens of people who came every day to ask for some of it. As we said before, history records the names of those who *served,* while the names of those who *were served* are forgotten. Considering that, isn't it strange that so many of us want to *be served* when we could *be serving*?

Generosity, thoughtfulness, and courtesy are examples of propriety that will never go out of style. These are lessons from water that show us more than a great way to self. They show us a way to live a memorable life.

Look back at the lessons we learn from water: fidelity, harmony, and propriety. We can't lose in selling if we have the gentle persistence and flexibility of water. The samurai said, "In battle I will dance your dance. If you move quickly, so will I. If you are slow and deliberate, I will be, too. I will take no absolute position that makes me rigid and difficult to work with, for what do I accomplish if I dance alone?"

EARTH

In addition to water, the samurai also learned from the earth. The earth represents permanence, a solid foundation under all we do. Yet we must study the earth in order to understand it, for the earth holds swamps that could be treacherous and caves where an enemy could hide. To ignore the lessons the earth teaches is to put your personal and professional life in danger.

Morihei said, "A good warrior-hunter must be able to melt into the landscape, become part of it, know it intimately, and respect it."

From the earth, the samurai learned love, service, compassion, and cherishing. Let's look at selling with these earth lessons in mind!

Love and Service

In addition to its romantic definition, love also means respect, devotion, kindness. As salespeople, we show this kind of love to our prospects when we seek to bring the best solution or product to meet their needs. Love means never offering products or solutions that won't work or won't solve the problem. Love means we can say, "This really isn't right for you. I wish it were." More often, it means that we'll devote the time needed to find out what the problem is before we start suggesting solutions.

Tale of a Modern Samurai

David, a friend of ours, recently went shopping for a microwave oven. He had never bought one before, so he went to a department store instead of a discount store because he wanted to learn all he could before deciding. The salesperson began by showing him a brochure of each model they sold and explaining all the technical features. The longer the salesman talked, the less David knew.

Next, David went to an appliance store, thinking, "These people are specialists so they'll help me figure this out for sure." The salesman there had apparently studied salesmanship with the lady at the department store, because he used the same technical approach.

By this time, David could have written a book on microwave ovens, but he still didn't know what to buy to meet his needs. On his way home he stopped by one more store. This time a samurai approached and asked if he could help. David replied, "I just need a microwave oven." The salesman simply asked, "Well, what do you cook?" David was amazed, because no one had asked him that before. He said, "I'll only use it to heat up my coffee in the morning and cook some Lean Cuisine if I get home late at night." The samurai, who had a comforting, grandfatherly manner, smiled and said, "Well, I could show you a half a dozen units, and all of them are first-rate. But if that's all you need it for, you should just buy this one! It's inexpensive, and it has all the features you'll ever need!" He took three minutes to explain why this was the right unit, and in another three minutes, David was on his way out of the store with the microwave under his arm.

Samurai, we all know, means "one who serves." The

world not only gives us a place to live our dreams, but the food to fuel our dreams as well. Giving needs to be at the heart of our selling. True love, after all, is all about giving. Doesn't the Scripture say that "God so loved the world that *he gave!*"?

Dr. Karl Menninger, founder of the famous Menninger Clinic, was once asked by a newspaper reporter what he would recommend to a patient who was suffering from depression. Menninger replied, "I'd suggest he go out his front door, go to the poorest part of town, and find someone to help. It's in *giving* of ourselves that we find happiness."

If you love your prospects, then serving them is no problem. You want to give your time, your talent, and your resources to help them fulfill their dreams and solve their problems. They will sense this and reward you for it with their trust, their confidence, and their business.

We once asked buyers to describe the best salesperson they ever worked with in just a few words. Here's what they said:

- There's just something about her. There's not one thing you can put your finger on, but she listens. She is genuinely interested in understanding exactly what it is that I want and need.
- He not only is concerned about service, he is concerned about your problems.
- This is going to sound really, really dumb, but there is a country-western song that I really like that kind of sums my favorite salesman up. It goes, "You gotta sing like you don't need the money. You gotta love like you'll never get hurt. You gotta dance like nobody's looking. If it comes from the heart, it'll work." With this guy, it comes from the heart.

Knowing the salesperson has your interest at heart makes the difference in any sale. And the more techni-

cal, complex, and expensive the sale is, the more important that "from the heart" feeling is.

Love your prospects, and they will love you in
return.

Emmet Fox wrote, **"Love is by far the most important thing of all.** It is the Golden Gate of Paradise. Pray
for the understanding of love, and meditate upon it
daily. **It casts out fear.** It is the fulfilling of the Law. It
covers a multitude of sins. **Love is absolutely invincible.**

**"There is no difficulty that enough love will not
conquer;** no disease that enough love will not heal; no
door that enough love will not open; no gulf that enough
love will not bridge; no wall that enough love will not
throw down; no sin that enough love will not redeem.

"It makes no difference how deeply seated may be
the trouble, how hopeless the outlook, how knotted the
tangle, how great the mistake, love and a servant's heart
can set it all right again. **If only you could love enough,
you would be the happiest and most powerful being
in the world."**[17]

Did Fox overstate the case? Just think of those who
have changed the world through love!

Compassion

Another lesson from the earth is compassion. Compassion is, if you will, love that has rolled up its sleeves and
gone to work to solve problems.

We've already looked at Tesshu's compassion for
people in need. Morihei's development of aikido, a
nonviolent form of self-protection, is an outstanding
example of love and peace applied in the midst of con-
frontation, chaos, and attack.

The Zhang River Annals gives this advice: "Whatever
you set your mind to do, you always should make the

17. From Emmet Fox, "The Golden Gate," in *Power Through
Constructive Thinking* (New York: HarperCollins, 1990).

road before you wide open, so that all people may tra-
verse it. This is the concern of a great man. If the way is
narrow and perilous, so that others cannot go on it, then
you yourself will not have any place to set foot either."

Compassion in selling is "making the road wide" so
your prospect can easily travel from problem to solution. The *Hagakure*, written in the twelfth century by a
samurai, says "Ill will...comes from a heart that lacks
compassion. If one wraps up everything with a heart of
compassion, there will be no coming into conflict with
people."

A Modern Samurai Shows Compassion

*Some years ago Karen called on a large, national account. She
waited patiently for nearly an hour in the lobby. The long
delay was perplexing because the prospect, whom we'll call
Dan, had seemed eager to meet with her when they set the
appointment. When Dan finally came into the waiting room,
he apologized profusely for making her wait. As they walked
together down the long corridor to his office, he explained that
he was delayed because of a doctor's appointment.*

"Nothing serious, I hope," Karen asked sincerely.

*He hesitated a moment and said. "I'm twenty-seven years
old, and the tests showed that I have a genetic disorder that
will take my sight in just a few years." As he spoke candidly
and matter-of-factly about his future, she listened with compassion and sympathy and then went on with her presentation.*

*A few weeks later, Karen came back to close the sale.
Since this would be the largest contract her company had ever
received, her company president came with her. As they drove
to Dan's office, she explained to the president that she had
seen a story on "60 Minutes" about a program of alternative
healing developed by Gerald Jampolsky at the Center for
Attitudinal Healing for children with terminal cancer.
"They've gotten some remarkable results not only with cancer
patients but with patients suffering from eye problems similar*

to Dan's," she said, "and I'm going to give him this little book about the program called Teach Only Love."

Her president couldn't believe what he was hearing. "Don't do it," he begged. "You'll blow the whole sale!" She stood her ground. "This is my client and my sale. I'm here to be of service, and I can think of no greater service than to try and save Dan's sight!"

When Dan came into the lobby, he walked across and gave her a hug. When they sat down in his office, she handed him the book and told him she just wanted to share that information with him in case it might help. Dan smiled at her and told her how much that meant to him. The president was holding his breath, but in less than an hour the sale was completed.

Did Karen take a chance at losing a sale? Perhaps. But her compassion and desire to serve were unquestioned, even outweighing her desire to make the sale. After all, no one cares how much you know u`ntil they know how much you care. She was saying to Dan, "I want to serve you as a *person*, not just as a client."

Cherishing

The earth also taught the samurai to cherish, for the earth herself must be cherished in order to remain fruitful. In the same way we should cherish our clients and the opportunities we have to serve them.

In the *Hagakure* it is written, "Above all, the way of the samurai should be in being aware that you do not know what is going to happen next and in querying every item day and night. You must cherish each opportunity as it comes along." In selling, we don't always know what is going to happen next, either. A new competitor springs up, the prospect's company is bought out, new technology comes along and makes whole industries obsolete almost overnight. Today, as much as ever, cherish the opportunity you have to serve. Cherish each client you choose to serve.

You must also cherish yourself. People who love and cherish themselves are then free to love and cherish the people they work with and the people they sell to. It does no good to "love your neighbor as yourself" if you don't love yourself! Buyers sense this depth of self-knowledge and confidence. Tesshu wrote, "Each person contains a boundless treasure within him- or herself. Yet, of all the billions of people on earth, how many are aware of their innate wealth? It is a great pity that people mistakenly value gold, silver, and diamonds rather than their own true riches."[18]

Cherish your company and its products or services; cherish yourself; cherish your prospects and clients—for they are true riches.

These lessons from the earth—love, compassion, and cherishing—separate superstar sales performers from the also-rans. If you serve your clients with these elements of the earth, you will experience an entirely different quality of life as a salesperson.

AIR

From the air, the samurai learned wisdom, light, and principle. Air became the symbol of the samurai's mind and spirit.

The early writings of the *Hagakure* put it this way:

Crystal clear,
sharp and bright,
my mind has
no opening for
evil to roost.

18. Stevens, *The Sword of No Sword*, p. 165.

Tesshu wrote: "All depends on mind. If one imagines the opponent to be skillful, the mind freezes, and the sword is held back; if one imagines the opponent to be weak, the mind is open, and the sword is unhindered. This is proof that nothing exists outside the mind. A swordsman may practice earnestly for many years, but if he is only moving the body and vacantly swinging the sword, his training is worthless. Outside the mind, there is no sword!"

The message is the same for us today as samurai salesmen. Selling is a battle of the mind and spirit, not a battle of products.

Let's look at these elements of the air that help us understand how to use our mind and spirit to be better at selling.

Wisdom

One of the greatest lessons taught by the air is the lesson of the beginner's mind, which we discussed earlier in Chapter 4. Probably no other concept so clearly conveys the samurai attitude about the mind.

"Throughout your life, advance daily becoming more skillful than yesterday, more skillful than today. This is never ending," wrote the author of the *Hagakure*.

The master Ganno once advised Tesshu, "If an opponent frightens you or confuses you, it means you lack true insight." To this Tesshu added, "Whenever the marvels of swordsmanship elude you, return to the beginner's mind."

The United Negro College Fund has an ad campaign that says, "A mind is a terrible thing to waste!" That is true, and it is also true that a *beginner's mind* is a terrible thing to lose! Have you ever seen a salesperson who has lost the beginner's mind? They are the people who know everything about everything. They have seen it all. Their conversations aren't vibrant and inquiring.

They're full of formulas, routines, answers, and stale stories. One of the greatest challenges to a long, successful career in selling must surely be to retain a beginner's mind. It's so much easier to find a groove, get in it, and mentally go to sleep.

There is nothing so deadly as a mind that was made up long ago and is no longer open to new data. "We acquire habits and no longer concentrate. Even when people give us coaching, then we protect our egos and cannot retrieve our Beginner's Mind," warns the author of the *Zen Way to the Martial Arts*.

Don't be narrow-minded, always looking for rules and recipes. Every situation requires its own reaction.

Light

Just as light penetrates the air, so it must penetrate our mind. The brighter the light, the more clearly the flaws in our world and our thinking appear. Have you noticed that some people only see the shadows? They only see what's wrong with their company, their products, and the marketplace. Remember Eeyore in *Winnie-the-Pooh*? Eeyore couldn't see the light if you blasted him with a spotlight. He always lived under a dark, gloomy cloud.

Go to the library and check out a copy of A. A. Milne's *Winnie-the-Pooh*, or better yet, purchase a copy.

Pooh came up to Eeyore, the grumpy old donkey, and said, "Good morning, Eeyore."

Eeyore's dark reply was in keeping with the lack of light in his life. "Good morning, Pooh Bear," said Eeyore gloomily. "If it *is* a good morning," he said. "Which I doubt."

Ever meet someone like Eeyore? Gloom and doom people aren't much fun to be around, are they? But all of us like to be around people who live in the light of enthusiasm and joyful anticipation.

Selling with light simply means that while you acknowledge the human shortcomings within your company and its current products, you believe that this is still the best way for your prospect to "light his way." You refuse to sink into the shadows. Any prospect likes a salesman who can, as the song says, "light up my life." If you can also light up his or her business, then so much the better!

Principle

The samurai also associated "principle" with air. Perhaps because, if you live in the light, it is so easy for people to see who you are and what you stand for.

"We must look after each other without regard to our own welfare, kill selfish desires, bravely face all enemies, and keep a stainless mind—this is the code of the warrior," the ancient samurai wrote.

Have you ever bought something, gotten it back home or to the office, and discovered it really didn't live up to its promise? How did you feel about the person who sold it to you? A truly principled person never overstates. When the samurai Morooka Hikoemon was called to swear before the gods on a certain matter, he said simply, "A samurai's word is harder than metal. Since I have impressed this fact upon myself, what further vow can I take?" In a simpler time, when someone wanted to talk about a person of integrity, he would say, "His word is his bond." When your word is your bond, or harder than metal, people will trust you, and they'll buy from you.

FIRE

For most of us today, the mention of fire evokes a lot of fear! Fear of loss of life and property. You can't remain passive around fire. It is the element that is clearly a call to action. That's why in our chapter on urgency, we quoted the samurai maxim, to "act as if a fire were raging in your hair!" Yet fire is also good. It is the fire of the sun that makes life possible on the earth, and the fires of winter allow us to survive until spring.

Fire reminded the samurai of three things: valor, progress, and completion. Let's look briefly at each.

Valor

Valor is an old-fashioned word that we hope will never go out of style. *Webster's* defines it as: "strength of mind or spirit that enables a man to encounter danger with firmness; personal bravery." *Valor* comes to us from the Latin *valere*, meaning "to be strong." So, though we don't use the word as often as we once did or probably should, its message is as powerful as ever.

Valor does not necessarily mean we are a Rambo, a valiant fighter. It means that we are firm and brave in the face of danger. Gandhi was a man of great peace, but he was nevertheless brave enough to face an armed adversary without flinching.

A warlord came to a monastery in Japan. The monks disappeared, leaving the master alone. The warlord walked up to him and demanded that the master should bow to him. The master politely refused. "I bow to no man," he said softly.

The warlord yelled, "Don't you know you are looking at a man who can run you through without blinking?" The master replied, "And you are looking at a man who can be run through without blinking." The warlord stared at him, bowed, and left.

What does it mean when we bring valor to bear in selling? It means we are brave enough to take risks. It means we have the courage to penetrate the account's needs and tell them what they need to hear, not merely what they want to hear.

We've shared many stories that attest to the bravery of the samurai. Now, we want you to imagine that you're an ancient samurai, well-versed in the "way of the sword." One day the Portuguese land, and for the first time you see the awesome power of firearms. Long before you can come close enough to engage the enemy with your sword, he can shoot his deadly missiles at you. (This is far, far worse than any competitive situation you've faced in selling, isn't it?) Well, what do you do? Do you worry and shrink back? Charge on, heedless of danger? Check the want ads for another line of work? Let's look at what the great samurai Tesshu did!

TALE OF THE ANCIENT SAMURAI

Tesshu considered his sword, which he called the *katasujin-ken*, the blade that protects and fosters life. Although he had never killed anyone, his sense of valor made him ready to give up his life at any time. He had conquered his fear of death. Once he was walking through the forest and met a hunter carrying a rifle. The hunter pointed the rifle straight at Tesshu and said, "Even a swordsman as skilled as you is no match for this gun." Without even a second's hesitation, Tesshu drew his sword and, with a ferocious yell, charged straight at the hunter! The hunter dropped his gun and ran away as fast as he could. The hunter's fear of death caused his defeat even though he had the "superior" weapon.[19]

We often work with salespeople who used to have the only product of its type on the market. Then, sud-

19. Adapted from Stevens, *The Sword of No Sword*, p. 38.

denly, a competitor appeared with a product even better! Ordinary salespeople often feel threatened, afraid, and confused. A samurai salesperson learns all about the new competitor and immediately devises a strategy to continue to win.

Ask yourself, "When do I turn and run? When do I allow the competitor to defeat me? When do I hesitate to make an important call, write a strategic letter, or contact the real decision maker?"

"If you open your hand, you can take hold of anything; if you close your hand, nothing can enter it," as *Zen Way to the Martial Arts* phrases it. The point is to open your mind to possibilities for success—that is the way of valor.

Progress

For the samurai, progress meant a life of study. The master swordsman Daishu said that your mind was no different from any other weapon in your inventory. "If a fine sword is not constantly polished," he said, "it will never show its luster. If you don't practice, you will never be able to master universals and particulars."

What are the "universals" and "particulars" a samurai salesman must master? To think and act with universal knowledge and wisdom is to keep the big picture in your mind. We must master the whole sales cycle, not simply the individual calls. Particulars are the details, the tactics, that must be mastered in order to fulfill the vision of the whole.

As we coach salespeople, we notice that some are great at strategy (universals) and yet are very poor at the tactics (particulars, that is, face-to-face selling). Others are just the opposite in their skills. It takes excellence in both to master the art of selling.

This focus toward progress is a good way of creating a fire, a burning passion for excellence every day, for penetrating life, not just skimming over it. Create this kind of fire in every area of your life: physical, love and family relationships, spiritual, as well as your career in sales. Don't allow any part of your life to coast. The weakness you allow in one area saps your strength elsewhere. When we lose a sense of *fire* and *progress* in any of these areas, our effectiveness diminishes. We stagnate. We become less than we ought to be. There's a country-and-western song that says, "You get what you settle for." Take a look at each area of your life and ask yourself if it has the sense of fire and progress you really want. If it doesn't, do something now! The point of power is now! You can only be powerful if you live today! *Full out! 100 percent!*

Recently we were at a company sales meeting as presenters were listing the strengths and weaknesses of their competition. We couldn't help noticing that not a single salesperson was taking notes. Later these same salespeople complained that they couldn't win because their competition was too strong. How ordinary! How un-samurai! Samurai salesmen don't ask life to come to them. They take responsibility. They take their foot off the brake and hit the accelerator.

"*Carpe diem*, seize the day! Penetrate your life! If you do, people will recognize that you are samurai. They'll want you on their team.

The samurai sword was known for its incredible sharpness, and some could cut through the barrel of a .30-caliber machine gun in one swipe. Yet the samurai knew that the blade was just a tool. It could only penetrate when wielded by a warrior with fire in his heart!

Fear quenches the spiritual fires of a samurai as surely as water quenches a physical fire. Don't let fear put out your fire!

Completion

Fire also reminded the samurai of completion. Fire was the crucible where the dross is burned away and their metal and their mettle were tested. The only way a samurai could become complete was to be a balanced person—and that required constant practice. A samurai practices alone. He practices against others. Especially, he practices regularly against the best of his competitors! The real competition, of course, is aimed at the prospect, because only the prospect can determine the winner of the battle.

Samurai hate to lose any competition. We know of one samurai who has found a unique way to deal with loss. Whenever someone else gets the sale, she immediately sends the prospect a direct-mail piece as if they had never met! She explained to her manager, "There are only two types of accounts: clients and prospects. Since they didn't become a client, they're now a prospect. They'll eventually come around, and next time I'll win the competition!" A samurai looks at a loss not as an end, but as a new beginning!

Let's look back at these four elements of nature and what they teach the samurai:

Water teaches fidelity, harmony, and propriety.
Earth teaches love, compassion, and cherishing.
Air teaches wisdom, light, and principle.
Fire teaches valor, progress, and completion.

The true art of samurai selling combines all of these elements. It is personal bravery along with compassion, iron discipline as well as a flexible response, determination combined with a great willingness to serve.

The challenge brought to us from these ancient warriors is to continue to look for our weaknesses . . . and make them our strengths! Look back through these lessons. Ask yourself, "In these elements, where am I the weakest? Am I afraid to really do the prospecting I need to do? Am I afraid to really qualify my accounts? Am I like a poorly trained swordsman, simply flailing around, thrashing through my territory? Am I trying to hide my weaknesses from my employer... and my prospects?" The true samurai knows that carrying weaknesses is like carrying big rocks around on his back. It only makes it that much more difficult to fight and win. The true samurai seeks balance and excellence in *every* area. That is your final challenge. That is the soul of the samurai.

CONCLUSION

WE HOPE THAT YOU DO NOT CONSIDER these lessons we have shared mere "tricks of the trade." They are not tricks. They are techniques and tools designed to help you change from the inside to become a samurai salesman, a salesman who seeks not to be served, but to serve. As a samurai salesman, your long sword is your desire to be of service. If your goal is to provide exciting solutions and exceptional service to your prospect, then there is nothing wrong with taking time to learn how to do it.

The value of any commodity goes up as the supply diminishes. In our world, however, gold is valuable, and many men and women work their entire lives just to acquire as much of it as they can. While we like money, too, if financial reward is your primary motivation, you will never be as successful or as happy as you could be. If you have truly acquired the mind of the samurai, other things will be more valuable to you, things like integrity, discipline, creativity, and fearlessness. Even these things will be focused in one direction: toward serving those you sell to.

Today most of the jobs in our country are service

jobs. Yet, as a nation, we provide notoriously poor service. These words are being written at five o'clock on a Tuesday afternoon. Two weeks ago a plumber came out and did some expensive plumbing underneath the kitchen sink. As he left, he told us how good his service was and that we would never have another problem with that sink. "If you should," be assured us, "I'll be right out to fix it." Saturday evening that fancy plumbing slipped loose, and the kitchen was flooded with water. We called the plumber, spoke to his answering machine, and are still waiting for a return call!

We have told this story to make this point: the more rare a commodity is, the more valuable it becomes. *Good service is a very rare commodity. In fact, the only thing rarer is legendary service!* Samurai provide legendary service!

If you are willing to truly be "one who serves," if you are prepared to provide legendary service, if you are prepared to discipline yourself so that you not only provide this kind of service but can convince prospects that you will provide it, there are no limits to what you can accomplish! When this happens, no competitor will be able to stand up to you or best you in a business battle.

Everyone wants to *be served,* but few want *to serve.* Yet no one is honored above those who serve. People remember those who serve long after they have forgotten those who were served. Does anyone recall where Einstein worked, the name of the drug company that first manufactured Salk's polio vaccine, the name of those who commissioned Beethoven's music, the pope who commissioned Michelangelo to paint the Sistine Chapel, the name of the tribe that was served by Albert Schweitzer, or the name of Mother Theresa's order? Probably not, because we forget those who were served, while we never forget "one who serves"!

Ordinary salespeople want to be served. Samurai salesmen want to serve. That's why samurai are in a class by themselves.

THE FINAL SECRET

You can be samurai. You now have all the tools you
need. Yet being a samurai is a journey and not a destination. The final secret is that if you have all the qualities we discussed except one, you are not yet a samurai. Examine yourself, and if you see a weakness in
your heart, dig it out, and make it your strength!
Wesley lacked faith, so he made faith his strongest asset.
Theodore Roosevelt was a weakling, so he established
a rigorous physical-fitness regimen and made physical
strength an asset. Einstein lacked understanding of
algebra, so he pretended x was a spy and made a
game of finding his true identity, becoming the greatest physicist of all time. Demosthenes had a harsh,
weak voice and taught himself to speak by reciting
while climbing mountains and talking above the roar
of the ocean with a mouthful of pebbles. Where are
you weakest? Find that area, and turn that weakness
into strength. That is what being a samurai is all
about; this effort is at the soul of every true samurai.

We know that you can do these things, but more
than that, we know that you *will* do these things,
because you have bought this book and read this far.
You have always had the desire to succeed in selling.
Now you have the knowledge. All that you must do
is known now, so nothing stands between you and
the success you deserve except time and persever-
ance.

We trust you will not consider this page the end
of your effort to become a samurai salesman, but the
beginning of a lifelong quest. As Shumryu Suzuki
said, "If your mind is empty, it is always ready for
anything; it is open to everything. In the beginner's
mind, there are many possibilities, but in the expert's
mind, there are few." A mind that is already filled
can hold nothing new.

In closing, let us say that we honor you for having begun a noble journey that will enrich you personally and professionally. We cherish you. We serve you—

for you are samurai!

For information on
The Samurai Selling System:

1 (800) 933–3187

Corporate Visions Inc.
774 Mays Blvd. #10
Incline Village at Lake Tahoe, NV 89451

SAMURAI SELLING SYSTEM

Power Demos

Workshop—A limited enrollment, 3-day workshop. Attendees are videotaped and personally coached on how to create and deliver product demonstrations and presentations that SELL. *(A variation of this workshop is designed for the unique presentation needs of executives.)*

Video Course—A self-study course that teaches you how to design and deliver powerful selling presentations and demonstrations. Kit includes a videotape, an audio tape, and workbook.

Sales Seminars

Samurai Selling System   (3-day seminar)

Creating a Sense of Urgency   (1-day seminar)

The Buyer's Mind   (1/2- day seminar)

Sales Samurai Videotape—A 25-minute videotape, designed to enhance sales meetings. The samurai, dressed in authentic samurai attire, vividly brings the samurai's message to today's salespeople. The samurai will motivate, challenge, and inspire your staff.

Corporate Visions would like to give special thanks to Marc Bockmon for his able assistance in the writing of this book. Marc is a Sales Samurai in his own right, and a professional writer of training, sales and safety programs. Marc Bockmon, Incorporated, can be reached through the Lloyd M. Jones Literary Agency at 1 (817) 483–5103.